contents

Introduction 1
Good practice in teaching reading
How to use this book

Section One   **The reading curriculum**   8
Reading to children   10
Recommended teaching approaches Reading aloud   10
Choosing texts to read aloud   11
Re-telling familiar stories   13
Recommended teaching approaches Vignette Year 1 Learning by heart   13
The power of song   14
Recommended teaching approaches Vignette Year R Hearing language patterns   15
Reading with children   17
Recommended teaching approaches Shared Reading   17
Teacher modelling: thinking aloud   17
Guided Reading   20
Assessment and grouping of children   21
Target setting   24
Planning for Guided Reading   25
Recommended teaching approaches Case Study Year R Guided Reading   27
Reciprocal reading   29
Evaluation   30
Reading by children   31
Independent Reading   31
Creating a supportive reading environment   32
Recommended teaching approaches Independent tasks   33
Reading at home   34

Section Two   **What the reading process involves**   36
Early concepts about print   37
Teaching print concepts   40
Teaching one to one correspondence   40
Recommended teaching approaches Vignette Year R Teaching print concepts   42
Teaching meaning   43
Recommended teaching approaches Vignette Year R Using meaning cues   44
Teaching structure - grammar   44
Teaching structure - punctuation   45
Recommended teaching approaches Vignette Year R Teaching grammatical structure and punctuation   45
Teaching visual information   46
Teaching phonics   46
The terminology of phonics   48
Recommended teaching approaches Graphic Information   49
Early progression in sources of information   51
Teaching reading strategies   53
Recommended teaching approaches Vignette Year R Cross checking self-monitoring and self-correcting   54
Teaching reading behaviours   56
Recommended teaching approaches Vignette Year R Developing fluency and phrasing   56
Children who experience difficulty with reading   57
Recommended teaching approaches Supporting children who are experiencing difficulties with reading   58

contents

	Section Three	**Comprehension**	59
		Moving to deeper understanding	59
		Structural features of text	59
		Vocabulary	60
		Prior knowledge or experience	60
		Grammatical skills	60
		Teaching reading comprehension	61
		Summarising	61
		Recommended teaching approaches *Vignette Year R* Summarising	62
		Vignette Year 1 Summarising	62
		Vignette Year 2 Summarising	62
		Predicting	63
		Recommended teaching approaches *Vignette Year R* Predicting	63
		Vignette Year 1 Predicting	63
		Vignette Year 2 Predicting	64
		Visualising	64
		Recommended teaching approaches *Vignette Year R* Visualising	64
		Vignette Year 1 Visualising	65
		Vignette Year 2 Visualising	66
		Questioning	66
		Literal questions	66
		Opinion-related questions	67
		Inferential questions	67
		Recommended teaching approaches *Vignette Year R* Questioning	67
		Vignette Year 1 Questioning	68
		Vignette Year 2 Questioning	68
		Connecting	69
		Recommended teaching approaches *Vignette Year R* Connecting	70
		Vignette Year 1 Connecting	70
		Vignette Year 2 Connecting	70
		Inferring	71
		Recommended teaching approaches *Vignette Year R* Inferring	71
		Vignette Year 1 Inferring	72
		Vignette Year 2 Inferring	72
	Section Four	**Assessing Reading**	74
		Types of assessment	74
		Assessment at different stages of reading progress	74
		What needs to be assessed?	75
		Collecting evidence	75
		Guided Reading records	75
		Running records	77
		Taking a running record	78
		Three levels of analysis of a running record	80
		Case study Assessing Bradley's and Suzy's reading - moving into instruction	82
		The phonics check	93
		In summary	93
		References	94
		List of children's books	96
		Glossary	98
		Appendix / Photocopiable resources	99

contents

List of Figures

Figure 1 The NLS Searchlights model of reading — 4
Figure 2 The Simple View of Reading — 4

Figure 1.1 A typical reading curriculum overview for Year 1, term 1 (first half) — 8
Figure 1.2 Example of Shared Reading as part of a unit of work (sessions 1 and 2) — 19
Figure 1.3 Book Bands with suggested targets — 22
Figure 1.4 Planning for a Guided Reading session - Reception — 26
Figure 1.5 Guided Reading Record for Blue Group — 29

Figure 2.1 Sources of information — 37
Figure 2.2 Early concepts about print: opportunities for assessment — 38
Figure 2.3 Early concepts about print: group assessment record — 39
Figure 2.4 Rimes that make nearly 500 words — 51
Figure 2.5 Early progression in sources of information for word identification — 52
Figure 2.6 Self-monitoring leading to self-correction — 53
Figure 2.7 Prompts for teaching reading strategies — 55

Figure 4.1 Assessment at each stage of the Early Reading continuum — 76
Figure 4.2 Running record sheet — 79
Figure 4.3 Conventions for annotating running records — 80
Figure 4.4 Bradley's running record assessment — 82
Figure 4.5 Suzy's running record assessment — 85
Figure 4.6 Summary of Bradley's and Suzy's assessments — 86
Figure 4.7 Blue group running record assessment summary — 87
Figure 4.8 Guided Reading planning for Blue Group — 88
Figure 4.9 Completed Guided Reading record for Blue Group — 89
Figure 4.10 Bradley's second running record assessment — 90
Figure 4.11 Comparison of Bradley's first and second running record assessments — 92

Teaching early reading: more than phonics

Introduction

Reading is a skill we use every day. Whether a road sign, or a novel, at the supermarket or the library, reading is an integral part of our lives. It is not merely a functional tool to meet the demands of society but a mechanism by which we can acquire knowledge and new ideas, gaining a greater understanding of the world around us. It opens the door to a feast of imagination and creativity which provides enjoyment to reader and author alike.

> *Reading is not just pronouncing written words. Children who become avid and accomplished readers focus on making sense from the start: they develop a habit of mind that expects the words they decode to make sense.*
> (Dombey et al., 2010:5)

As long ago as 1998 the National Literacy Strategy (DfEE, 1998), through the Framework for Teaching, introduced the notion of the Searchlights model of reading (Figure 1). This represents the reading process as involving four strategies or 'searchlights'. In this model, readers use four sources of knowledge to support decoding and understanding of the text:

- phonic knowledge (sounds and spelling)
- grammatical knowledge
- word recognition and graphic knowledge
- knowledge of context.

Left: Figure 1 The NLS Searchlights model of reading

By 2006 the government had introduced the concept of the 'simple' view of reading (Gough and Tunmer, 1986: Rose, 2006). Gough and Tunmer emphasised that decoding and comprehension must both be present if children are to read for meaning. Rose (2006) expressed this diagrammatically (see Figure 2) as a means of identifying differences in the balance between decoding and comprehension.

Below: Figure 2 The Simple View of Reading

However, reading is not a 'simple' task. Word identification may well involve comprehension, particularly where words such as 'read' or 'sow' are involved. And reading is, of course, much more than word identification. It is a complex interaction between reader and writer that requires children to develop a range of information, strategies and behaviours which they can use independently, a knowledge and understanding of the world and a rich and broad vocabulary that they can bring to texts they read.

If children are to progress as readers, schools will need to provide key elements of good practice. At the heart of this is a strong emphasis on oral language development, which is particularly crucial in the early stages of reading.

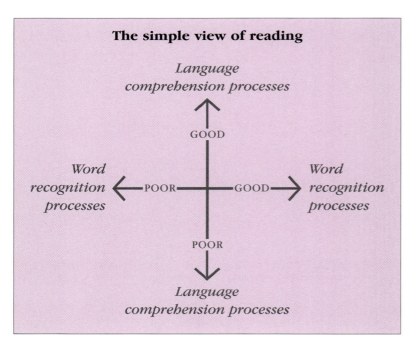

introduction

Good practice in teaching reading

Good practice includes highly trained, effectively deployed staff with sound subject knowledge, a consistent approach across each year group and throughout the school and quality resources which are well organised. In addition, good practice requires rigorous assessments which are used effectively, daily reading sessions based on assessed needs and close monitoring of the assessment and teaching of reading throughout the school. Storytime, reading to children, literacy rich environments, including book corners, also play a key role and a high level of parental involvement is essential.

Learning to read should not be regarded as a hierarchy of skills from lower to higher order, but as a developmental language process. The approaches in the initial stages will colour the children's motivation and their perception of reading as a purposeful and valuable activity. (Clark, 2014:12)

Underpinning all of these elements, there needs to be a broad and rich reading curriculum which engages teachers and children alike - a curriculum which builds on children's own experiences and interests, makes use of the environment and fosters an atmosphere in which all languages, dialects and traditions are valued - a curriculum that promotes a positive reading ethos throughout the school.

Language is the tool through which ideas are stored in memory. For these reasons oral language is the basis of interpreting print. As a general rule anything children have difficulty saying cannot be easily read. There is usually a close relationship between a child's growth in oral language and his [sic] progress in reading. (Hildreth, 1959: 566)

In line with these principles for good practice, this book is designed to fit with the national curriculum for English which stresses skilled word reading involving 'both the speedy working out of the pronunciation of unfamiliar printed words (decoding) and the speedy recognition of familiar printed words' (DfE, 2014: 14) in partnership with knowledge of language, and of the world, to support comprehension. The approach to comprehension in this book aligns with the NC statement that:

Comprehension skills develop through pupils' experience of high-quality discussion with the teacher, as well as from reading and discussing a range of stories, poems and non-fiction. All pupils must be encouraged to read widely across both fiction and non-fiction to develop their knowledge of themselves and the world they live in, to establish an appreciation and love of reading, and to gain knowledge across the curriculum. (DfE, 2014: *ibid*.)

national curriculum

introduction

While many children in the UK bring knowledge of a language - or languages - other than English, the teaching suggestions work equally well with bi-/multilingual children or English first language speakers and the advice to parents has been developed in multilingual communities.

> *For the first five years the child's language growth is entirely dependent on what people say to him [sic] – on how much they speak to him [sic], about what things, in what dialect or language and in what manner, whether gentle and explaining or peremptory and imperative.* (Clay, 1991: 70)

Each section of the book is designed to align with - and enhance - the reading requirements of national curriculum. However, although the national curriculum follows a year-by-year programme, the underlying view of this book is that learning to read is best seen as a developmental continuum, not necessarily tied to year groups.

This book offers practical guidance to those wishing to provide a full rich reading curriculum for children whilst ensuring that they meet the statutory requirements of the national curriculum for English. For that reason, although the curriculum emphasises phonics teaching and learning, the material presented here goes well beyond that element in taking a holistic view of what becoming a reader involves. This view is founded on three key elements in the reading process:

> *A balanced approach means… ensuring that classrooms are filled with interesting written texts – on screen as well as on paper – and that children are given rich experiences to put these texts to use.* (Dombey et al., 2010:7)

semantic (meaning), syntactic (sentence structure) and graphophonic (sound symbol correspondence). All these **sources of information** need to be systematically taught to support children to:

- understand that reading has to make sense
- gain knowledge of sentence grammar and punctuation
- get to grips with visual information – the print on the page (grapheme/phoneme correspondences and other letter patterns including high frequency words)

as well as developing a range of **reading strategies** and **behaviours**.

How to use this book

Each section deals with essential parts of provision for reading. It need not be read in any particular order.

The first section **The reading curriculum** gives an overview of all aspects of teaching reading.

Section Two gives the details of **What the reading process involves**, from early concepts about print through to developing fluency.

Section Three **Comprehension** looks at all the skills needed for successful understanding, with vignette examples of sessions for each of Reception, Year 1 and Year 2 to support teaching.

The final section **Assessment of reading** provides step-by-step guidance for keeping informed assessments and records of progress.

Throughout the book there are key teaching points, some of them vignettes, drawn from examples of good practice and key questions to help focus on providing good practice. A glossary of terms is supplied at the end of the book.

introduction

Sources of Information for word identification

Meaning (semantic: pictures and context)　　　　*Does it make sense?*

Structure (syntactic: grammar and punctuation)　　*Does it sound right?*

Visual (graphophonic: phonics and graphic representation)　　*Does it look right?*

Strategies (processing information)
- self-monitoring
- self-correcting
- re-reading
- reading on
- cross checking
- searching for more information
- orchestrating all sources of information.

Behaviours
- understanding that English print goes left to right
- reading fluently without finger pointing
- reading longer phrases and more complex sentences
- reading silently most of the time.

Sources of information, strategies and behaviours also support understanding.

Acknowledgements

I should like to acknowledge permission to use material developed by Barking and Dagenham Primary and Secondary English Teams. Material from the Reading Recovery Programme, developed in New Zealand, England and the USA have been an important source in putting this book together. Many thanks to all those people who have extended my knowledge and influenced my thinking, particularly my colleagues Sue Matthews, Jo Smith and Gill Stringer, for their generosity in sharing ideas so freely. Thanks are also due to Sue Bodman, Henrietta Dombey and Angela Hobsbawm for their helpful comments and to Seren Freestone, Rebecca Kennedy, David Reedy and Carolyn Swain. Especial thanks to Eve Bearne.

section one the reading curriculum

The reading curriculum

The national curriculum for English is clear about the value of reading as it 'feeds pupils' imagination and opens up a treasure-house of wonder and joy for curious young minds' (DfE 2014:14). The national curriculum also aims to ensure that all pupils:

national curriculum
- *read easily, fluently and with good understanding*
- *develop the habit of reading widely and often, for both pleasure and information*
- *acquire a wide vocabulary, an understanding of grammar and knowledge of linguistic conventions for reading, writing and spoken language*
- *appreciate our rich and varied literary heritage.* (DfE, 2014:13)

In order to pursue these aims, any rich reading curriculum needs to encompass three key elements:

reading *to* children

reading *with* children

and reading *by* children.

These elements need to be present for all children regardless of their developmental stage, in order for them to progress as readers.

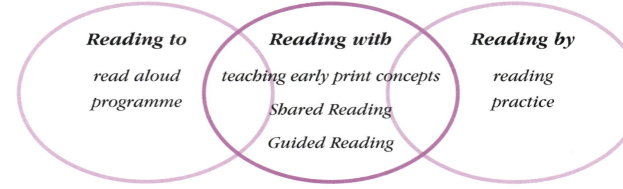

Figure 1.1 gives an example of a typical reading curriculum overview for Year 1, term 1 (first half).

A useful phonics programme is *Letters and Sounds* which can be accessed on https://www.gov.uk/government/uploads/system/uploads/attachment_data/file/190599/Letters_and_Sounds_-_DFES-00281-2007.pdf

section one

Strand	Week 1　　Week 2　　Week 3	Week 4　　Week 5　　Week 6
Reading with **Whole Class** *Units of work*	**Transition from YR** Reading familiar stories - including favourites from YR **3 x 45 minutes per week**	**Picture Books** Shared Reading and Writing: Role Play into Writing units: *Traction Man is Here* by Mini Grey *Monkey and Me* by Emily Gravett *Mr Gumpy's Outing* by John Burningham
Reading with Phonics including sentence level work		**Phonics programme** Including the teaching of high frequency words, predictable phrases and sentence structures **5 x 20 minutes per week**
Reading with Guided Reading		**Guided Reading** Groups and related tasks **20 minutes sessions**
Reading by Independent reading tasks		**Independent tasks** **20 minutes sessions within Guided Reading time**
Reading to Read Aloud Programme 5 x 15 minutes per week	**Picture Books Poetry** A range of favourite picture books, poems and rhymes enjoyed in Year R Texts linked to the role play area theme	**Picture Books Poetry** A range of poems and rhymes Other books by Mini Grey, Emily Gravett and John Burningham

Figure 1.1 A typical reading curriculum overview for Year 1, term 1 (first half)

section one the reading curriculum

Reading to children

Much has been written over time about the joys of reading to children. Teachers often talk about children being 'spellbound' as they read aloud to them.

national curriculum — *An important aim of the national curriculum is to develop pupils' 'love of literature through widespread reading for enjoyment.'* (DfE, 2014: 13)

To achieve this aim the benefits of reading aloud to children can never be underestimated. It plays a pivotal role in developing children's reading enjoyment and engagement from the earliest stages of pre-school to the more developed stages of Year 6 and beyond.

Every time we read to a child, we're sending a 'pleasure' message to the child's brain. (Trelease, 2013:6)

Reading aloud to children develops their understanding of how narrative works. They come to recognise that stories have plots, characters and settings. They also gain a familiarity with written language, which is very different from spoken language. Even books for young children use language that is denser, less rambling and has differently structured verb and noun phrases. When children are read to, they can hear and internalise these grammatical language structures and therefore begin to bridge the gap between the written and spoken word, something many children find difficult.

Reading aloud enables children to develop an increasingly rich and broad vocabulary which they can then apply to their own reading and writing. It is an opportunity for them to hear fluent, phrased and expressive reading. Above all, it allows children to engage in texts beyond their instructional level and so provides them with opportunities to access more varied and complex language.

national curriculum — *Pupils should have extensive experience of listening to, sharing and discussing a wide range of high-quality books with the teacher, other adults and each other to engender a love of reading at the same time as they are reading independently.* (DfE, 2014:12)

Recommended Teaching Approaches
Reading aloud

When reading aloud to children, in order to create deeper understanding of a text, it is important to consider:

- Familiarity with the story: the teacher needs to know the story well before reading it to children to enable the children to take deeper meaning by reading with expression and embellishing the text.
- Interaction with the audience: enhancing the meaning through body language, facial expression, vocal expression (including tone of voice, pitch and volume), pace of reading.
- Telling or reading? Alongside reading aloud to children, oral retelling of stories is also important. Retelling stories changes the relationship or interaction between the teacher and the children. It offers the teacher opportunities to change stories to alter nuances, mood or overall meaning, to manipulate vocabulary and introduce new or alternative word choices that may not be contained within a written a text.

section one

- Places to ad lib: this enables the teacher to make connections with what children already know or need to know, re-introduce new vocabulary and make sure the children understand elements of the story.
- Personalisation: making connections with text and personal experiences can enhance understanding.
- Making text-to-text connections: have the children come across stories with similar settings?
- Prediction, anticipation and suspense building: all these contribute to children's understanding of story structures.
- Questioning: prepare a range of questions to help children understand, for example, character motivation/cause and effect (see Section Three page 66). Some questions should also be generated by the children.
- Using illustrations: images not only enhance meaning, they can tell more of the story than just the words or, indeed, tell a different story from the words.

Choosing texts to read aloud

It is crucial that any read aloud programme should include quality texts, carefully selected for maximum impact. The use of quality texts ensures that children become engaged and develop a positive attitude to books and reading.

First Week at Cow School by Andy Cutbill, ill. Russell Ayto (2011) Harper Collins Children's Books. ISBN: 9780007274680

Owl Babies by Martin Waddell, ill. Patrick Benson (1996) Walker Books. ISBN: 9780744549232

The Adventures of The Dish And The Spoon by Mini Grey (2007) Red Fox. ISBN: 9780099475767

Rosie's Walk by Pat Hutchins (1998) Red Fox. ISBN: 9780370324463

The Rainbow Fish by Marcus Pfister, trans. J.Alison James (1998) North South Books. ISBN: 0038332606140

section one the reading curriculum

Criteria for the choice of literary texts

Types of text	What do they offer?	Examples
Texts with subtleties, for example, that are multilayered and stand exploration, re-reading and raise genuine questions.	help children learn how to read for inferences – between the lines and behind the images.	*Rosie's Walk* by Pat Hutchins *Tadpole's Promise* by Jeanne Willis *Cat on the Mat* by Brian Wildsmith
Texts that will engage children including those with intriguing plots and those with a range of structural features, for example captions, labels, flaps, typography.	support children's deeper understanding of texts and foster an enjoyment of reading.	*Leon and the Place Between* by Graham Baker-Smith *The Naughty Bus* by Jan Oke *The Adventures of the Dish and the Spoon* by Mini Grey
Texts that can be read aloud. *NB It is easy to assume that all story books are good to read aloud but some language structures and story plots can make taking meaning difficult, for example comic book formats don't lend themselves to reading aloud.*	allow children to access material beyond their instructional level, support the development of vocabulary and understanding of grammatical structures. foster enjoyment of reading.	*Don't Let the Pigeon Drive the Bus* by Mo Willems *Whatever Next?* by Jill Murphy *The Rainbow Fish* by Marcus Pfister
Texts that are representative of personal experience and a range of cultural traditions.	help children to make text-to-self connections and enable them to bring their own experience to the text, supporting reading comprehension.	*Handa's Surprise* by Eileen Browne *Lima's Red Hot Chilli* by David Mills *The Bear Under the Stairs* by Helen Cooper
Texts which challenge • language • feelings • attitudes • relationships • scenarios represented.	support reading comprehension beyond the literal requiring children to make text-to-self connections to bring deeper understanding to the text. provide opportunities for evaluative comments.	*John Brown, Rose and the Midnight Cat* by Jenny Wagner *Not Now Bernard* by David McKee *Farmer Duck* by Martin Waddell
Texts that provide good models for writing *NB Complexity of plot can get in the way of providing good models.*	support the writing process through enabling children to use simple plots, characterisations and settings in their own writing.	*The Rainbow Fish* by Marcus Pfister *Elmer* by David McKee *The Pig in a Pond* by Martin Waddell *Leon and the Place Between* by Graham Baker-Smith

section one

Using texts that meet these criteria enables teachers to work on a range of reading comprehension strategies at different levels. After teachers have read aloud, children invariably want to revisit those texts during independent sessions.

> ### Key question
> Which quality texts have you and your colleagues found invaluable for reading aloud? It might be worth developing a list to be shared - and adding to it as new favourites come to light.

Re-telling familiar stories

Encouraging children to re-tell familiar stories enables them to internalise a variety of story patterns, giving them an understanding of how narrative works, and to practise and rehearse a range of skills. When children write a story they know well they can focus on technical skills such as use of punctuation, the use of added detail or the use of connectives to link ideas. Once children know a simple story, they can elaborate, change details and make the story their own.

Recommended Teaching Approaches

Vignette Year 1 *Learning by heart*

This Year 1 teacher used Quentin Blake's *Mrs Armitage Queen of the Road* as a basis for her class exploring the story and learning it by heart. The children had read other Mrs Armitage stories, so were familiar with the characters and style of writing. She followed a 6-Step process to build their knowledge of the story and confidence as storytellers:

Step 1 *Read the story and discuss characters, events, and vocabulary*

The teacher read the story a few times and the children naturally joined in with some of the key phrases in the text. They then explored Mrs Armitage's character by hot seating and role on the wall and sorted out the storyline by different groups freeze framing the episodes.

Step 2 *Create key visuals which may help with the retelling*

The teacher and teaching assistant created a big car picture (with parts that fell off at key moments in the story) to aid the children's development of specific vocabulary and also to use when telling and retelling the story.

Step 3 *Learn to retell the story*

The teacher selected parts of the story to read and repeat, asking the children to join in. In line with her usual practice, she accompanied this step with simple signing, mime and other actions as she has found this effective before in helping the children recall events and vocabulary when they are retelling the story on their own.

Step 4 *Create a story map*

The children were familiar with story maps from previous work but this time the teacher had prepared junk modelling materials for children, in groups, to make 3D maps of the storyline. They then used these to help them remember key events as they began to tell the story to each other in pairs.

Step 5 *Practise*

The teacher gave the children plenty of time to act out the story and tell it to their partners using the 3D story map. In preparation for writing their own versions of the story the children drew pictures of their favourite episodes.

Step 6 *Write own version of story*

Once the children had a good grasp of the story structure, the teacher asked them to write the story from Breakspear's point of view (Mrs Armitage's faithful dog). She was pleased to see that as they wrote their stories they used storytelling language, repetition of particular phrases and varied vocabulary and that they were confident about the events.

Later in the year the teacher used the same process as a frame for the children to write a sequel to *Mr Gumpy's Outing* by John Burningham.

national curriculum *Through listening, pupils also start to learn how language sounds and increase their vocabulary and awareness of grammatical structures. In due course, they will be able to draw on such grammar in their own writing.* (DfE, 2014: 21)

The power of song

Alongside reading aloud and oral retelling of stories, sits the power of song. Learning songs, and lots of them, supports the development of the skills needed before or during 'formal' reading instruction. It could also be said that learning songs supports the reading process way beyond the early stages. Many songs tell stories and by learning and internalising them, children can develop skills of reading comprehension such as summarising, visualising, connecting and inferring (see Section Three page 61). Some songs, of course, provide even greater support for the development of reading comprehension in a similar way to books, films or artefacts. Perhaps this is more so as children develop as readers and begin to tackle more complex themes. Because children learn songs off by heart they are able to internalise the story patterns - they learn about how stories are structured, how characters might look, feel and think and how settings can be integral to the story.

In songs where the verses are in series, for example, 'Farmer in the Dell', the story moves on quickly without the reinforcement of a chorus. Songs with choruses usually further reinforce the meaning behind the story, for example 'Jamaica Farewell'. In this case, the chorus repeats the sorrow of the central character leaving Kingston. Songs offer the chance to talk with children about character, as in 'Mary Had a Little Lamb' or thoughts and feelings as in 'You are my Sunshine'. Settings, too, are an important part of songs, for example, 'Morningtown Ride'; they allow children to visualise and make connections with their own lives (text-to-self connections see page 69). Although some songs do not tell stories, for example 'The ABC song' or counting songs, they have other positive functions in developing early reading, like sequencing.

Not only do songs help develop children's reading comprehension, but they also develop their sources of information (meaning, structure and visual information - see page 37) all of which are vital in supporting independent decoding skills. Children will come to know that as they sing, the song needs to make sense (or nonsense!) in the same way as when they read. They will use the repeated patterns (both rhythmic and verbal), choruses and repeat refrains to support their understanding of grammatical structures in English, especially in the early stages of reading development where texts contain many repeated patterns. In addition, pitch and tone support sound discrimination which is linked to phonological awareness. For example, the contrast between a deep voice and a high voice, a high note and a low note, a loud bang and a soft tap, a drum and a triangle, is important if children are to discriminate between particular letter sounds. Tone also supports the reading of punctuation, for example, at a question mark the pitch of our voice goes up.

Learning and internalising songs also helps develop reading behaviours, in particular fluency and phrasing. (It is highly unlikely that children will sing hesitantly!) As their repertoire grows and becomes more familiar, they will be able to hear what fluent story language sounds like.

Just as children need daily stories to develop as readers, so, too, they need daily songs: songs, and rhymes that they become familiar with and internalise. Text and song combined present a particularly powerful model, as this Year R teacher found. Learning the song supported the children's understanding of the text.

In year 1:

Pupils should be taught to develop pleasure in reading, motivation to read, vocabulary and understanding by learning to appreciate rhymes and poems and to recite some by heart. (DfE, 2014:20)

In year 2:

Pupils should be taught to develop pleasure in reading, motivation to read, vocabulary and understanding by continuing to build up a repertoire of poems learnt by heart, appreciating these and reciting some, with appropriate intonation to make the meaning clear. (ibid.:27)

national curriculum

Recommended Teaching Approaches
Vignette Year R *Hearing language patterns*

As part of her teacher assessment during Guided Reading, a Reception teacher noticed that some children were finding difficulty with simple repeated grammatical structures that they encountered in their early reading texts. For example:

Here is the cat.
Here is the dog.
Here is the goat.

This was especially so when the sentences became longer. For example:

Look at me, I am reading.
Look at me, I am painting.

She decided, as a daily part of her work, to revisit familiar songs with the children. She selected songs with strong, yet simple rhythmic patterns such as 'Twinkle Twinkle Little Star' and encouraged children to join in and use hand actions and/or clapping to reinforce the rhythm. During these sessions the teacher would start with a familiar song. This daily repetition allowed the children to internalise the patterns quickly and almost without thought. She would then introduce a new song thus building the children's repertoire.

In a later session the teacher introduced a new song 'Do Your Ears Hang Low?' In this more complex song, the rhythmic patterns are slightly syncopated and although repeated, are more difficult for children to internalise. With this in mind, she initially asked the children to sing at a slower pace in order for them to hear how the patterns changed. This fed into their reading as the texts they were encountering had longer grammatical structures with some subtle changes. For example:

Where are you going?
Where, oh where are you going?

The teacher noticed that the impact on the children's reading was almost immediate. They soon had little difficulty hearing and recalling simple, repeated patterns on a consistent basis.

The composite features of songs include many characteristics shared with narrative texts.

section one the reading curriculum

Aspects of songs	Example	Features	Sources of information
Words (stories)	'Jamaica Farewell' 'Mary had a little lamb' 'Go Tell Aunt Rhody' 'Miss Polly'	Narrative Rhyming narrative	Meaning
Timbre	'Scarborough Fair' 'Donna Donna'	Moods and feelings	Meaning
Choruses	'Cera Cera' 'Jamaica Farewell' 'The Grand Old Duke of York'	Re-emphasise plot Repeated patterns	Meaning Structure
Refrains	'Bought me a cat' 'The wheels on the bus' 'Old MacDonald' 'The Three Bears'	Repeated patterns	Structure
Rhythms	'Long time girl' '(Come on and) Join in the game' 'Fancy Anansi'	Repeated patterns	Structure
Pitch	'Sing a Song of Sixpence' 'The Prehistoric Animal Brigade'	Sound discrimination	Visual
Tone	'Donna Donna' (minor key) 'The Music Man'	Sound discrimination	Visual

section one

Reading with children

A balanced reading programme will include a variety of reading experiences, levels of support and methods of instruction including Shared, Guided and Independent reading.

While Shared Reading gives an opportunity for whole class teaching, Guided Reading is a group approach that supports children while they work with others of similar ability with the same book.

Recommended Teaching Approaches
Shared Reading

Shared Reading can be carried out either during whole class or group sessions using an enlarged text which the teacher introduces and reads with the children. The text is usually shared over a number of days and forms an integral part of the teaching sequence in any unit of work. In the early stages, children will often join in refrains or familiar parts of the book. Shared Reading provides the opportunity to model how to read - as well as how pleasurable it is to read. During Shared Reading, the teacher provides a high level of support focusing on any vocabulary that might challenge the children and talking about using a range of comprehension strategies to deepen understanding of what is being read. It is a time for exploration.

Teacher modelling: thinking aloud

Teacher modelling of reading can articulate aspects of the reading process, explicitly demonstrating key strategies or behaviours, for example, fluency and expression or one-to-one correspondence for early readers. In teaching comprehension it is vital that teachers articulate the thinking process, for example, predicting: *'I think that the animals won't come back to the mat because they were frightened by the cat.'*

> 'Think aloud' is about 'making the implicit thinking process explicit for her pupils, allowing them to improve their comprehension by understanding how and why a reader uses strategies.' (Courtney and Gleeson, 2007: 63).

Elements of modelling/thinking aloud:

- Identify the strategy you want to focus on, for example, predicting, inferring…
- Select an appropriate text for the strategy and decide on a specific passage that will offer a good example of the strategy.
- Review the text and decide where you will stop to explain your thinking process.
- Before reading, explain to the class the strategy you are going to use and why it is useful. This will allow the children to identify the strategy more easily when you use it.
- Read the passage and model the identified strategy using Think Aloud. It is important to have considered what you will say before you start reading so that the language you use is clear and concise.
- After you have read the passage, talk over with the children where you used the strategy and how it was useful. (adapted from Courtney and Gleeson, 2007).

Shared Reading gives the teacher a chance to model the cadences of book language and reading fluently with expression; it also gives them a chance to introduce children to a range of different authors, illustrators and picturebook makers. And, of course, sharing a book (or other text), whether with a whole class, a small group or just one child is a very pleasurable experience.

Reading activity

- The teacher selects, introduces and reads with the children.
- The same text is shared over a number of days.
- Children may join in refrains or parts if they feel confident.

section one the reading curriculum

What happens
- Teaching primarily focuses on comprehension alongside early print concepts, sources of information, strategies and behaviours.
- Teaching can also draw attention to features of print, layout, vocabulary, meaning, grammar and visual information as part of the reading process.
- There is a high level of oral interaction with the teacher.
- The teacher provides a high level of support and uses a wide range of questioning skills.

Why it is valuable

Shared Reading:
- provides support from the class
- provides opportunities for supported participation, e.g. talk partners
- allows children to access texts beyond their instructional level
- helps to develop a sense of genre
- explicitly demonstrates reading behaviours, e.g. one to one correspondence
- encourages children to develop a full range of reading strategies
- allows for specific teaching of sources of information.

What is needed
- Big books
- Enlarged texts
- Photocopied extracts
- Multimodal texts, e.g. picture books, film,
- Images
- Props
- Paintings

Figure 1.2 gives an example of Shared Reading as part of a Year 1 unit of work on book making.

Right: Figure 1.2 Example of Shared Reading as part of a unit of work (sessions 1 and 2)

section one

Year 1, Term 1 Unit of Work – Role play with writing

Unit of work	Genre	Audience	Drama work
Making a book based on *This is the Bear and the Scary Night*	Stories with familiar settings	The class	Role play techniques Tableaux Freeze frame

Objectives

Develop pleasure in reading, motivation to read, vocabulary and understanding through:
- retelling stories ordering events using story language
- identifying the main events, characters and settings in stories
- exploring familiar themes and characters through role play
- relating events to personal experience
- using key features of narrative in their own writing
- orally composing and writing simple sentences.

Teaching Sequence	Before Session 1	Session 1	Between sessions 1 and 2	Session 2
Introduction/focus Whole class teaching Shared Reading Teacher demonstration *Oral interaction: teacher/pupil; pupil/pupil* Shared Writing Teacher scribe *Supported composition: oral and/or written* Independent work Plenary conclusion	*Collect and display a series of books with familiar settings for read aloud programme.* *Make characters (bear, boy, owl, man, other man) for retelling.* *Collect props (bear, chair, owl, trombone) for role play.*	**Shared Reading** • Read through text without interruption. Read through again getting children to join in the rhyming words at the end of each line. • Explain to the children that the story is set in the park. • With talk partners, ask children to generate ideas about what they might see in the park. Scribe on flipchart. • Use tableau technique to form the setting. • Retell the story asking some children to be the characters. • Embellish the story using descriptive words and phrases to describe the park.	*Display texts and props for children to retell.*	**Shared Reading** • Re-read the story encouraging children to join in with rhyming words at the end of each line. • Recap from previous session discussing where the story is set. • Retell the story using characters emphasising key events within a simple narrative structure. *NB do not retell using rhyme.* • Ask children to join in with the sound effects, for example, the hooting of the owl, splash in the pond.

section one the reading curriculum

Guided Reading

Guided Reading gives children the opportunity to develop skills and strategies which they can then use flexibly and appropriately to comprehend as they read. It is a key teaching strategy for improving children's reading fluency, comprehension and response. Guided Reading helps overcome barriers to learning so that children become confident in using a range of strategies to get meaning out of a text. Equally, Guided Reading should encourage children's enjoyment of being readers.

The aim of every Guided Reading session is to encourage and extend independence. Texts are selected to match the reading ability of the group. They should be unfamiliar or unknown and present some challenge to the reader. As opposed to an individual approach to teaching reading, Guided Reading provides a significantly higher degree of instruction time for each child. Groups of children work together on the same text so that support is drawn not only from the teacher but from other members of the group, through a combination of discussion, thinking out loud and reading. While working with the group, the teacher gives focused attention to individuals as they read whilst the rest of the group continue to read to themselves.

> *The goal of Guided Reading is to develop a self-extending system of reading that enables the reader to discover more about the process of reading while rereading. As children develop these understandings they self-monitor, search for cues, discover new things about the text, check one source of information against another, confirm their reading, self-correct and solve new words using multiple sources of information.* (Iaquinta, 2006:414)

Reading activity

- Teacher considers the instructional level of the group through benchmark and other assessments (see Section Four page 74).
- Teacher selects text to teach sources of information, strategies and behaviours and to focus on aspects of comprehension and vocabulary.
- Teacher introduces the text and any unfamiliar vocabulary and engages children's prior knowledge.
- Children read the text to themselves.

What happens

- Teacher introduces the text and encourages discussion and response.
- Teacher demonstrates sources of information, strategies or behaviours as appropriate.
- Children read and problem solve new text in a way that is mostly independent.
- Early readers vocalise while teacher 'tunes in' to individuals in turn.
- Fluent readers read silently vocalising only at the teacher's given signal.

Why is it valuable

- Text and its use are closely matched to the needs and abilities of the children.
- Text challenges the reader at an instructional level 90 - 94% accuracy (see Section Four page 80).
- Allows the teacher to teach a variety of reading skills.
- Provides the teacher with the opportunity to observe how each child progresses.

What is needed

Individual books in sets (at least six) which could include:

- Reading scheme books appropriate to the developmental level
- Non-scheme books
- Short novels
- Poems.

The Guided Reading Cycle lasts the course of half a term at the end of which the children's progress is evaluated.

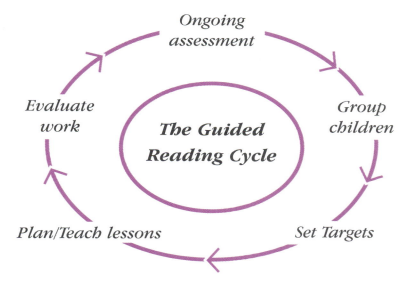

Over a year, teachers will need to balance the types of reading experiences, selecting from as wide a range as possible of information texts, stories, poems. They will also know their year's objectives for teaching reading and the age-related expectations for their class. The starting point will be assessment data and ongoing records of the children's reading ability and so it is important that they know where the children are on the reading continuum - whether they are Emergent, Early, Transitional or Self-extending readers (see pages 22-23). This information will help the teacher to decide on groupings. As reading abilities change, so groups will need to be adapted to ensure that the Guided Reading session addresses the particular needs of each child.

Assessment and grouping of children

Prior to Guided Reading instruction, teachers will assess the children in order to put them into groups. It is important to note that a child may not benefit from a Guided Reading approach until some early print concepts are in place, for example, knowing how a book works, knowing that there are such things as letters and that they can be clustered to make words, knowing about first and last letters and matching letters one to one (see Section Two page 37). In the early stages of reading, when children are still developing decoding skills, assessment initially takes the form of running records (see Section Four page 77). The children are then grouped according to ability and need. However, decoding skills alone are not the only guides to reading progress; there may be occasions when the teacher works with the children in a strategic way, for example, using mixed ability groups where there is a need to develop fluency or certain aspects of comprehension.

Running record assessments (see Section Four page 78) should be carried out at the beginning of the Autumn Term. Subsequent assessments should be based on teacher assessment carried out during Guided Reading sessions. The exception to this is for children who appear to have made little or no progress, in which case further, perhaps regular, running records need to be carried out and analysed by the teacher.

section one the reading curriculum

Figure 1.3 Book bands with suggested targets.
Adapted from Bodman and Franklin *Which Book and Why* (2014)

Band 1 Emergent readers	Band 2 Early readers	Band 3 Early readers	Band 4 Early readers	Band 5 Early readers
Examples of texts *At the Zoo* *Dressing Up* *Mum* *I go to School* (Nelson Thornes) *Ice Cream* (Pearsons)	**Examples of texts** *The Baby Owls* *Ben's Treasure Hunt* *Father Bear Goes Fishing* *Hedgehog is Hungry* (Nelson Thornes) *Making Pizza* (Gardner Education)	**Examples of texts** *Baby Bear Goes Fishing* *Lucky Goes to Dog School* *Sally's Beans* *The Hungry Kitten* (Nelson Thornes) *How Many Legs?* (Pearson)	**Examples of texts** *The Best Children in the World* (Kingscourt) *Honey for Baby Bear* *Tom's Ride* *Come on, Tim* (Nelson Thornes) *Floating and Sinking* (Gardner Education)	**Examples of texts** *Duma and the Lion* *The Gingerbread Man* *The Ugly Duckling* (Pearson) *Greedy Cat's Door* (Gardner Education) *Houses and Homes* (Nelson Thornes)
Characteristics of texts • Small amount of text - one short sentence. • Picture cues very supportive of the text; in repeated language patterns the word changed is well supported by the picture. • In repeated language patterns the word changed is in the same place on the page - often the last word in the sentence. • 25-40 highest frequency words.	**Characteristics of texts** • Increasing amount of text - 3-5 lines. • More interpretations of the pictures are needed. • Some book language is used. • Punctuation beyond the full stop is used, for example, speech marks, commas and question marks. • Increasing number of high frequency words. • 50-90 words.	**Characteristics of texts** • Pictures less supportive of text although unusual vocabulary is well supported. • Introduction of present and past tenses. • Longer structures which are not always repeated. • Changes in word order of two word phrases e.g. 'said mum', 'mum said'. • Increasing range of punctuation, e.g. italics. • Most complex high frequency words, e.g. 'away', 'will', 'comes'. • More appropriate to take words apart, e.g. 'in', 'sh', 'ed'. • 100 - 150 words.	**Characteristics of texts** • Pictures only partially support changes in repeated language patterns. • Pictures can be used to make inferences. • Text is in different places - layout is different. • Range of tenses used. • More complex sentences which go across lines. • Introduction of subordinate clauses. • More varied punctuation, e.g. apostrophes on possessives and contractions. • More varied text features, e.g. bold print. • 150 plus words.	**Characteristics of texts** • Illustrations provide limited support. • Events sustained over several pages. • A lot more information to be obtained from the text. • More literary language used. • Varied longer sentences which are not repetitive. • Mixture of sentence lengths. • A variety of tenses used. • 250 plus words.
Targets • Cross check meaning with visual information, initial letter sound. • Read, on the run, a small number of high frequency words. • Read without finger pointing most of the time. • Recall some simple events in stories. • Make simple predictions before reading. • Make text-to-self connections.	**Targets** • Cross check meaning with visual information beyond the initial letter sound. • Cross check meaning with structure especially for repeated patterns. • Read, on the run, an increasing number of high frequency words. • Match 1:1 consistently. • Recall some simple events in stories. • Make simple predictions before reading. • Make text-to-self connections.	**Targets** • Begin to orchestrate meaning, structure and visual information at the point of error. • Control longer grammatical structures. • Take words apart and confirm with meaning and structure. • Read fluently, without finger pointing. • Recall some simple events in stories. • Make predictions before and during reading. • Make text-to-self and text-to-text connections.	**Targets** • Re-read and read on to orchestrate all sources of information. • Use context cues to support predictions of unfamiliar words. • Read fluently, longer passages of text, including speech. • Recall events in stories. • Make predictions before and during reading. • Make text-to-self and text-to-text connections.	**Targets** • Re-read and read on to orchestrate all sources of information. • Use context cues to support predictions of unfamiliar words. • Read fluently, longer passages of text, including speech. • Recall and sequence key events in stories. • Make detailed predictions before and during reading and support views. • Make text-to-self and text-to-text connections. • Use information in texts to find specific facts.

section one

Band 6
Early readers

Examples of texts

Jack and the Beanstalk (OUP)
Toby and the Big Tree (Nelson Thornes)
Are you my Mother? (Collins)
The Kick-a-lot Shoes (Kingscourt)
Gorillas (Gardner Education)

Characteristics of texts
- Different genres in each book.
- More print than pictures.
- Different print devices are used such as bold text.
- More literary language used.
- Structures more complicated.
- Length of sentence and the position on the page varies.
- Contractions and inflections are used widely.
- 250 -300 words.

Targets
- Re-read and read on to orchestrate all sources of information.
- Use context cues to support predictions of unfamiliar words.
- Read fluently, longer passages of text, including speech.
- Make detailed predictions before and during reading and support views using context and characterisations.
- Make text-to-self and text-to-text connections.
- Use information in texts to find specific facts.

Band 7
Transitional readers

Examples of texts

The Cabin in the Hills
The Race to Green End (Nelson Thornes)
The Sleepover (Pearson)
Chicken Licken (Collins)
Interesting Insects (Kingscourt)

Characteristics of texts
- More complex episodes in stories and events.
- Little support from illustrations.
- May have full pages of print.
- More use of literary language.
- More unusual and challenging vocabulary.
- Non-fiction texts contain more formal sentences.
- 300 plus words.

Targets
- Re-read and read on to orchestrate all sources of information.
- Read fluently, longer passages of text, including speech.
- Make detailed predictions before, during and after reading and support views using context and characterisations.
- Make text-to-self and text-to-text connections.
- Use information in texts to find answers to simple questions.

Band 8
Transitional readers

Examples of texts

Star Boy's Surprise (Collins)
The Pied Piper of Hamelin (OUP)
The Hare and the Tortoise
Rex Plays Fetch
Hippos (Nelson Thornes)

Characteristics of texts
- More complex episodes in stories where plot reflects the feelings of the writer.
- Still some illustrations.
- Some books with chapters for more sustained reading.
- Characters more developed.
- Wider vocabulary and range of terminology.
- Non-fiction texts cover a wider range and contain different text features.

Targets
- Re-read and read on to orchestrate all sources of information.
- Self-monitor, search and self-correct.
- Read fluently, longer passages of text, including speech.
- Make detailed predictions before, during and after reading and support views using context and characterisations.
- Make text-to-self and text-to-text connections.
- Infer meaning from the text.
- Use information in texts to find answers to simple questions.

Band 9
Transitional readers

Examples of texts

The Very Smelly Dragon (Pearson)
Basil's Night Out (Kingscourt)
Trapped!
Seven Foolish Fishermen
Horses (Nelson Thornes)

Characteristics of texts
- Story plot more complex and reflects the feelings of the writer.
- Still illustrated but some books with chapters.
- Characters more developed.
- Wider vocabulary and range of terminology.
- Sentence structures becoming longer and more complex.
- Non-fiction texts cover a wider range and contain different text features.

Targets
- Re-read and read on to orchestrate all sources of information.
- Self-monitor, search for more information and self-correct consistently flexibly and automatically.
- Read fluently, longer passages of text, including speech.
- Make detailed predictions before, during and after reading and support views using context and characterisations.
- Make text-to-self and text-to-text connections.
- Infer meaning from the text.
- Use information in texts to find answers to simple questions and relate to prior knowledge.

Band 10
Self-extending readers

Examples of texts

Hansel and Gretel (Pearson)
Hatupatu and the Birdwoman
Earth Materials (Kingscourt)
Nelson is Kidnapped
Holiday at Lighthouse Rock (Nelson Thornes)

Characteristics of texts
- Wider range of genres and writing style.
- Story plot more complex and sustained.
- Still illustrated but some books with chapters.
- More than one point of view expressed in text.
- Characters more developed.
- More metaphorical or technical language used.
- Wider vocabulary and range of terminology.
- Sentence structures longer and more complex.
- Non-fiction texts contain more detailed information and have a wider range of text features.

Targets
- Re-read and read on to orchestrate all sources of information.
- Self-monitor, search for more information and self-correct consistently flexibly and automatically.
- Read fluently, longer passages of text, including speech.
- Make detailed predictions before, during and after reading and support views using context and characterisations.
- Make text-to-self, text-to-text and text-to-world connections.
- Infer meaning from text.
- Use information in texts to find answers to a broader range of questions and relate to prior knowledge.

section one the reading curriculum

Target setting

Having assessed and grouped the children, it is important to decide what the 'next steps' will be, as these targets will inform the specific teaching focus over the half term.

The targets must be based on the evidence from the assessments carried out. However, as a result of the analysis, several different issues may arise. For example, a child may be neglecting meaning, be over reliant on visual information, at the same time as finding self-monitoring difficult. It is important, therefore, for teachers to make professional judgements about what focus will have the most effect.

In the early stages, the targets that tend to move children's reading forward are those focused on reading strategies and comprehension.

Targets can be selected from a range of reading continua, but the banding system *Book Bands for Guided Reading* produced by the Reading Recovery National Network provides the most comprehensive guidance. Full listings are available on the CDROM accompanying *Which Book and Why* (Bodman and Franklin, 2014). The listing provides information on a gradient of challenge of more than 3,000 texts organised into 11 bands. The bands represent a developmental continuum which is not necessarily related to year groups although generally bands 1-4 would reflect the normal range of achievement within Reception; in Year 1, bands 2-7 represent the normal range and in Year 2, bands 5 -11 would cover the normal range, although they suggest that generally Year 2 children would not read beyond band 10. Bodman and Franklin point out, however, that there may be a wider range of achievement in any class so that schools will need to make arrangements for children whose achievement falls below or exceeds the ranges indicated. They also point out:

> *Because of the variety of texts and topics covered and the subjective nature of decisions involved in banding text, you may not always agree with us about the challenge offered by books in certain bands. Our advice is that you should always take into account your own experience and knowledge of your children, and use the banding simply as a guide.* (Bodman and Franklin, 2014: 103).

Figure 1.3 gives some examples of books for each band, their characteristics and suggested targets, from the Emergent and Early stages to more complex texts for more Self-extending readers at the end of Key Stage 1 and into Key Stage 2. For many more examples of books and guidance see *Which Book and Why*. Some texts mentioned as examples may place greater demands on readers especially at the earlier stages of development. They are usually more complex in a variety of ways including plot, vocabulary and text features (layout, typography etc.) and work best when there is a focus on reading comprehension (reciprocal reading) rather than decoding. Some examples of these texts would be *Not Now Bernard* by David McKee (Band 5), *The Very Hungry Caterpillar* by Eric Carle (Band 6), *The Pig in the Pond* by Martin Waddell (Band 7), *Grace and Family* by Mary Hoffman (Band 8), *Princess Smartypants* by Babette Cole (Band 9) and *Dogger* by Shirley Hughes (Band 10).

See previous page for *Figure 1.3 Book bands with suggested targets.* Adapted from Bodman and Franklin *Which Book and Why* (2014).

Planning for Guided Reading

With the targets for the group determined, it is important to plan a series of focused Guided Reading sessions for the half term. Lessons should last between fifteen and twenty minutes depending on the level and difficulty of the text the children are reading. The selection of appropriate material to meet the targets is crucial to the success of Guided Reading planning and teaching.

Children should have opportunities to access a range of texts. Books included should be selected from a wide range of material including reading schemes and non-scheme titles. It is not ideal to be 'faithful' to one scheme as children can become over-dependent especially on the repeated grammatical structures and vocabulary contained within them. (See Appendix for a photocopiable Guided Reading Planning and Target Setting format.)

Planning for Guided Reading should include:

- the names of the children in the group
- the instructional level at which they are reading
- the targets identified for instruction
- the texts selected for each session
- examples of prompts to support teaching.

It will also take into account all elements of the reading process: sources of information, strategies and behaviours (see Section Two page 37 for full explanation):

Sources of Information for word identification

Meaning (semantic: pictures and context)	*Does it make sense?*
Structure (syntactic: grammar and punctuation)	*Does it sound right?*
Visual (graphophonic: phonics and graphic representation)	*Does it look right?*

Strategies (processing information)

- self-monitoring
- self-correcting
- re-reading
- reading on
- cross checking
- searching for more information
- orchestrating all sources of information.

Behaviours

- understanding that English print goes left to right
- reading fluently without finger pointing
- reading longer phrases and more complex sentences
- reading silently most of the time.

Sources of information, strategies and behaviours also support understanding.

A Guided Reading session follows this sequence:

section one the reading curriculum

Lesson Section	Teaching/Activities	Prompts
Book introduction **Orientating reader to text**	Generate questions. Look at tricky words and new vocabulary. Ask children to make predictions. Identify points of potential difficulty (the 'trick' of the book, for example, particular grammatical structures and sometimes typography or structural features such as pop-ups, flaps, etc.).	*This book is about* (short synopsis/overview) *Today we are reading a…book* (name text type) *Look at the cover…what do you think this is about?* *Does anyone know other books about…?* *What do you think might happen?* *Now I'm going to show you the trick of the book.*
Teaching to targets	Teach to chosen targets.	*Support teaching to targets, for example:* *Does that make sense?* *If it was…what letter would we see at the beginning?* *Get your mouth ready to make the first sound.*
Independent reading	Prompt for use of sources of information, strategies and behaviours, as targeted. Praise to confirm behaviours. Observe and monitor closely.	*Did that make sense?* (sources of information) *How did you check if you were right?* (strategies) *Make your reading sound like a story.* (behaviours)
Return to the text	Praise for use of sources of information, strategies and behaviours, as targeted. Remodel or demonstrate. Generate questions for comprehension (literal and inferential). Prompt for personal response to the text.	*I liked the way you….* *I liked the way you read this part…* (name a specific example and specific behaviour) *Listen to me read this bit, what do you notice?* *You thought … would happen. Were you right?*
Follow up activities	Re-reading text independently. Reading with a partner. Retelling with visuals, puppets etc. Home/school reading Text marking Activities relating to text, for example, word games, comprehension.	• *Read the story again with a partner.* • *Can you find evidence for…?* • *Match these little words we found in the text.*

section one

In year 1:

By listening frequently to stories, poems and non-fiction that they cannot yet read for themselves, pupils begin to understand how written language can be structured, such as how to build surprise in narratives, and the characteristic features of non-fiction. (DfE, 2014: 20)

In year 2 children should have opportunities for:

... listening to, discussing and expressing views about a wide range of poetry (including contemporary and classic), stories and non-fiction at a level beyond that at which they can read independently. (ibid.:27)

national curriculum

Recommended Teaching Approaches
Case Study Year R *Guided Reading*

Jan, a Reception teacher, identified targets for Guided Reading with Blue Group:

- Cross check meaning with visual information
- Read fluently - two and three word phrases.
- Read an increasing number of high frequency words in context.
- Make text-to-self connections.

Figure 1.4 Planning for a Guided Reading session - Reception

Guided Reading Record

Targets	Class / Group / Half Term / Texts	Prompts
1. Cross check meaning with visual information. 2. Read fluently - two and three word phrases. 3. Read, on the run, an increasing number of high frequency words. 4. Relate events in stories to personal experiences (text-to-self connections)	**Class** Ladybirds **Group** Blue group **Half Term** Autumn first half **Texts** *Lazy Pig* *The Merry-go-round* *Sally and the Daisy* *Lizard Loses his Tail* *A Home for Little Teddy* *Tom is Brave*	• What would make sense and look right? • Look at the picture, then at the word. • Make your reading sound like a story. • Run the words together. • Is that a little word you know?

Name	Session 1	Session 2	Session 3	Session 4	Session 5	Session 6	Returning to the text
Suzy A.							
Bradley E.							
Angelica D.							
Eddie R.							
Roshan J.							

section one the reading curriculum

Figure 1.4 shows her planning. At the beginning of the session Jan orientated the children to the text by showing them a range of small world farmyard animals. She encouraged responses by getting the children to make connections with any experiences they had of visiting a farm, asking them:

> *Have you ever been to a farm?*
>
> *What other animals might you see?*

Selecting one or two animals she asked the children:

> *What noise does it make?*

After some discussion about farm animals Jan gave a brief synopsis of the text explaining that the pig in the story was lazy and that is why it was called *The Lazy Pig*:

> This is a story about a farm where lots of animals live. It is early in the morning and the sun has come up. The first animal to get up is the rooster (showing the children a small world animal of the rooster) and he is going to wake the other animals up by saying 'cock-a-doodle-doo' (pointing this out in the text). But the pig was lazy and he didn't want to get up. I wonder why? (the children offer ideas). In the end he is so hungry he gets up for his breakfast.'

Jan was then able to move into the teaching segment of the lesson. She referred the children to page 11 of the text, having initially covered the word 'asleep' with a sticky note. The children then made suggestions as to what the word might be. Prompting the children she asked:

> *'Look at the picture. What would make sense?'*
>
> *'If it was "sleeping" what letter would I see at the beginning?'*

The children were able to refer directly to the picture (meaning). Jan then revealed the letter enabling the children to select the word that made sense and looked right at the beginning.

Using magnetic letters, board and word cards, she selected two high frequency words 'said' and 'the' from the text. The children read the words off the card, built them with the letters, and finally located them in the story. She then distributed the texts and the children read independently while she listened to them in turn, making notes on the Guided Reading Record (Figure 1.5.)

Rounding off the lesson, Jan praised the children for the accurate reading of high frequency words and cross checking. She then selected one example of cross checking in order to reinforce her previous teaching.

As a follow up activity, the children then retold the story using the small world animals in the outdoor sand area.

Section Four (page 82) shows how Jan assessed the children's reading using her Guided Reading notes and running records.

section one

29

Guided Reading Record

Targets	**Class** Ladybirds	**Prompts**
1. Cross check meaning with visual information. 2. Read fluently - two and three word phrases. 3. Read, on the run, an increasing number of high frequency words. 4. Relate events in stories to personal experiences (text-to-self connections)	**Group** Blue group **Half Term** Autumn first half **Texts** Lazy Pig The Merry-go-round Sally and the Daisy Lizard Loses his Tail A Home for Little Teddy Tom is Brave	• What would make sense and look right? • Look at the picture, then at the word. • Make your reading sound like a story. • Run the words together. • Is that a little word you know?

Name	Session 1	Session 2	Session 3	Session 4	Session 5	Session 6	Returning to the text
Suzy A.							
Bradley E.							
Angelica D.							
Eddie R.							
Roshan J.							

Figure 1.5 Guided Reading Record for Blue Group

Reciprocal reading

Reciprocal reading is about:

Sharing and discussing texts.

Engaging in dialogue and activities which require re-reading, thinking and open ended discussion.

Exploring texts and responding creatively to what is read. (Goodwin, 2014)

As young readers develop, the Guided Reading lesson sequence might vary and could move towards children being engaged in sessions of the sort carried out in the 'reciprocal reading' programme (Palincsar, 1986). These are interactive, child-led discussions that may not include actual reading at all during the session. Although elements of reciprocal reading will occur in sessions at the early stages of reading, it is important that children are taught a full range of word identification skills before they access the full reciprocal reading format. Reciprocal reading aims to improve reading comprehension, often through the strategies of predicting, questioning, clarifying and summarising. These strategies will be modelled by the teacher and applied during routine reading sessions. Although reciprocal reading focuses on these strategies, they should be part of a broad and rich reading curriculum which also aims to develop: previewing, self-questioning, making connections, visualising, knowing how words work, monitoring, summarising and evaluating.

section one the reading curriculum

Evaluation

At the end of the half term a summative assessment will be made of each group, taking account of the following:

> [C]hildren use metacognitive strategies to generate their own questions about the text, to relate their own knowledge to the new knowledge posed in the text, to summarise what they have learned and to identify what they found confusing in the text and how they might proceed to render the text more meaningful. The teacher proceeds, with deliberate intention, to enable the children to acquire knowledge about reading and themselves as readers that will be useful to them.
> (Palincsar et al., 1993: 55)

- Have the children all met the targets set?
- Were some targets only partially met?
- What targets need to be set for the next half term?
- Do any children need to be moved into a different group?
- Do further assessments need to be made?

See Section Four for full details of assessment in Guided Reading.

Key question

How do you and your colleagues share ideas about the most successful approaches to Shared and Guided Reading?

It might be worth collating these as part of your policy documentation.

With thanks to Westlands first school, Droitwich, Worcestershire.

section one

Reading by children

As with any skills learnt, children need opportunities for Individual Reading to practise and consolidate their learning. Time needs to be built into the school day for children to read and enjoy books independently. Teachers need to direct independent reading activities to ensure all children have reading practice time. This can be done as part of the Guided Reading independent tasks when pupils can be directed to the reading area within the classroom. There also need to be some undirected opportunities where the children can enjoy texts of their own choice. A full range of texts should be made available including 'special' book boxes of texts previously read aloud to children so that they can be revisited. The reading area or book corner within a classroom is crucial in building a positive reading ethos in the early stages.

> **national curriculum**
>
> All pupils must be encouraged to read widely across both fiction and non-fiction to develop their knowledge of themselves and the world in which they live, to establish an appreciation and love of reading. (DfE, 2014: 14)
>
> During year 2, teachers should…make sure that pupils listen to and discuss a wide range of stories, poems, plays and information books. (*ibid.*: 26)

Independent Reading

Independent reading is an integral part of any balanced reading programme.

It provides opportunities for children to practise the skills they have been taught in class.

Independent reading can be either directed or undirected by the teacher.

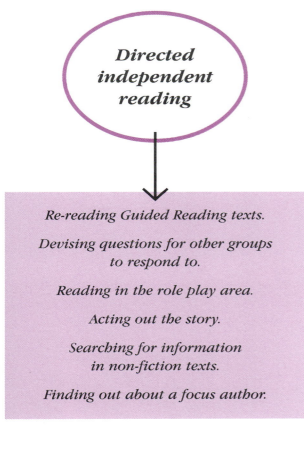

Directed independent reading

Re-reading Guided Reading texts.

Devising questions for other groups to respond to.

Reading in the role play area.

Acting out the story.

Searching for information in non-fiction texts.

Finding out about a focus author.

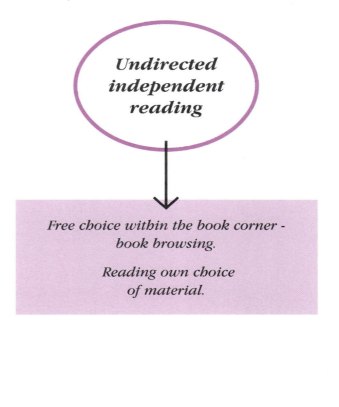

Undirected independent reading

Free choice within the book corner - book browsing.

Reading own choice of material.

section one the reading curriculum

Creating a supportive reading environment

Text Resources

- Fiction books including picture books and short stories, big books, browsing books and read aloud books
- Story DVDs
- Non-fiction books on a range of subjects
- Reference books like encyclopaedias
- Poetry and rhymes
- Song books
- Dual/parallel text books in different languages
- Plays
- Children's own books (from shared writing)
- Flap/pop-up books
- Wordless books
- Comics, magazines and newspapers
- Big books
- Joke books

Other resources

- Good book display - trolleys, shelving
- Carpets
- Cushions
- Soft Chairs
- Boxes and baskets for different categories of books
- Author focus boxes and displays
- Puppets - characters from books etc.

With thanks to Gascoigne primary school, London Borough of Barking and Dagenham.

section one

Recommended Teaching Approaches
Independent tasks

While the teacher is engaged with the group of children, the remainder of the class will be working on a range of reading-related tasks. In the early stages of reading development, children will work on activities which reinforce concepts covered during the Guided Reading session, including comprehension. The activities can take place in indoor or outdoor settings, independently or with another adult.

As children develop as readers, independent tasks will increasingly require them to read in pairs and groups and discuss parts of a text, generate questions, text mark evidence from the text, make notes and prepare for the Guided group discussion. Independent activities can be done in pairs or individually, for example:

- Asking groups to devise questions for other groups to respond to.
- Reading in the role play area and act out the story.
- Playing prepared games, or word level activities with magnetic letters.
- Searching for information in non-fiction texts.
- Finding out about a focus author.
- Partnered reading.
- Focusing on character:
  - think up questions you would like to ask a character in preparation for hot-seating
  - write letters between two characters in the book - this can be an effective a paired activity with each child taking the role of one character.
- Focusing on plot/events:
  - draw a story map
  - retell the story orally using story props
  - write a 'next section' of the story.
- Focusing on the book as a whole:
  - design a new cover for the book
  - prepare a page for reading aloud
  - work on computer activities linked to the book
  - make masks or puppets or dress paper dolls to represent the book characters to act out key episodes.

Key question

How do you and your colleagues plan for individual reading practice and ensure all children have opportunities to read independently?

With thanks to Dorothy Barley infant school, London Borough of Barking and Dagenham.

section one the reading curriculum

Reading at home

Reading at home provides vital opportunities for reading practice, allowing for development beyond the classroom setting. The home environment, where all members of the family are involved in reading, is a rich resource which not only supports children's reading development at school but also encourages them to enjoy reading for pleasure. Children who are encouraged to listen to or read stories in their home languages are further advantaged as they come to understand how language works in more than one context. They have, in other words, more than one point of reference, particularly in terms of meaning. Other advantages for bilingual children are more wide-ranging and include the development of communication, cognition and social interactive skills.

Parents or carers, older siblings or other family members should be encouraged to read with the children daily. Books should be sent home regularly along with a reading card or journal in which a family member can make comments about the child's reading. Sessions to help family members can be very helpful in forging links between school and home over reading.

In the early stages of reading development, reading at home should take precedence over any other form of homework. A typical home/school reading card might look like this:

HELENSVILLE PRIMARY SCHOOL **HOME/SCHOOL READING CARD**  *Name* _____ _____ *Class* _____ _____	**Suggestions for reading at home** Here are a few suggestions to make reading with your child enjoyable: **Do** • Make sure that the atmosphere is relaxed and happy and that your child enjoys the time together. • Let your child sit with you. • Keep the session short. • Read as often as you can find the time. Try to read every day. • Give plenty of praise. • Read with (not just to) your child. It is often more fun to read a page together or take turns with each sentence. • Let your child read at their own pace. • Encourage your child to make attempts at any words he or she can't read. • Tell your child the beginning sounds if he or she doesn't know them. If this still doesn't help, just tell them the word straight away, and carry on reading. Don't make an issue of it. • Look at and discuss the pictures. • Talk to your child about the book. • Feel free to ask for help and advice or simply discuss your child's reading. **Try not to:** • Make reading an unpleasant task or a chore. • Have the television on during the session. • Make your child feel he or she is in competition with anyone else.

section one

Key question

How do you and your colleagues support family members in knowing how best to encourage enjoyable reading at home?

It might be worth noting these approaches as part of your policy documentation.

section two what the reading process involves

What the reading process involves

Skilled word reading involves both the speedy working out of the pronunciation of unfamiliar printed words (decoding) and the speedy recognition of familiar printed words. Underpinning both is the understanding that the letters on the page represent the sounds in spoken words.
(DfE, 2014:14)

Once they have the early print concepts in place, (see page 37), children can move into what it known as 'formal' instruction. There are three key components of reading that children need to be systematically taught in order for them to be able to process print: sources of information, strategies and behaviours.

Sources of Information for word identification

Meaning (semantic: pictures and context)	*Does it make sense?*
Structure (syntactic: grammar and punctuation)	*Does it sound right?*
Visual (graphophonic: phonics and graphic representation)	*Does it look right?*

Strategies (processing information)
- self-monitoring
- self-correcting
- re-reading
- reading on
- cross checking
- searching for more information
- orchestrating all sources of information.

Behaviours
- understanding that English print goes left to right
- reading fluently without finger pointing
- reading longer phrases and more complex sentences
- reading silently most of the time.

Sources of information, strategies and behaviours also support understanding.

Figure 2.1 shows the relationships between the sources of information - the 'item' knowledge that children require:

- meaning: understanding that reading has to make sense
- structure: knowledge of grammar and punctuation - how language is written on the page
- visual information: phonological and graphic.

Alongside this information, children need to develop a range of reading strategies such as re-reading, reading on and cross checking. They will need to develop reading behaviours - fluency, expression and intonation - in order to become competent, independent readers. Teacher modelling is invaluable here (See Section One page 17).

section two

MEANING
pictures and context
(semantic knowledge)

knowledge of the story
knowledge about the world or events
knowledge of vocabulary

Does it make sense?

STRUCTURE
(syntactic knowledge)

knowledge of grammar
and punctuation

oral language
knowledge of how to construct
sentences orally

Does it sound right?

TEXT

VISUAL
sound and spelling (graphophonic)

knowledge of sounds   **graphic knowledge**
ability to go from letter to sound   word chunks, endings (e.g. ing, ed)
ability to blend phonemes   analogy (e.g. book, look)
                   big/little words
                   high frequency words

Does it look right?

Figure 2.1 Sources of information

Early concepts about print

Before children move into the 'formal' instruction of processing print independently, early reading behaviours, or concepts about print, need to be developed. Many children will come to school with some of this knowledge firmly in place. They may well already know where the front of a book is, which way up a book will go or even where to start reading. It is, therefore, important to assess children's knowledge of print concepts so that teaching can reflect their needs rather than repeating, unnecessarily, concepts they already know.

Opportunities for assessing print concepts will arise within the everyday activities of the classroom. These assessments are often most effectively done through observations carried out by the teacher or another adult during small group work and Guided Reading sessions. Shared Reading and observations of children reading independently also offer opportunities to assess children's understanding of print concepts. Figure 2.2 lists early print concepts with prompts that can elicit information and the types of activities most conducive to assessments and Figure 2.3 provides a grid for recording observations during group work.

section two what the reading process involves

Early Concept	Prompts	Assessment Opportunities
Recognise one or two words in different contexts.	• Can you find your name? • Is that a little word you know?	• Finding names, e.g. register, pegs, name cards, names on alphabet • Flash cards - whole class/school assessment • Reading written texts
Understand and use simple terminology such as book, right way up, front, back, upside down.	• Put the book on the stand. • Show me the front of the book. • Take a book from the table.	• Shared Reading • Individual Reading • Observations
Understand that print goes from left to right including return sweep.	• Where do I start to read? • Show me where to start reading. • Where do I go after that?	• Shared Reading • Individual Reading • Shared Writing
Understand that the left page comes before the right. *NB print must be on both pages when assessing this.*	• Where do I start to read? • Show me where to start reading. • Where do I go after that?	• Shared Reading • Shared Writing
Know that print (not the picture) tells the story.	• Where do I start to read? • Show me where to start reading. • Where do I go after that?	• Shared Reading • Individual Reading
Know that there are letters, and clusters of letters called words.	• Show me the first letter. • Show me the last letter. • Show me a capital letter. • Show me one word.	• Using magnetic letters to make words - put words into context • Shared Reading • Individual Reading • Shared Writing
Understand that there are first letters and last letters in words.	• Show me the first letter. • Show me the last letter. • Show me a capital letter. • Show me one word.	• Shared Reading • Guided Reading • Individual Reading
Match one to one.	• Point to the words as I read them. • Match the counters to the words. • Use your pointing finger.	• Individual Reading (using the pointing finger) • Group/Guided Reading • Cut up sentences • Moving counters to match words

Figure 2.2 Early concepts about print: opportunities for assessment (drawn from the work of Marie Clay)

section two

Early concepts about print *Group assessment record*

Date _____

Group _____

Early Concept	Name	Name	Name	Name	Name	Name	Name	Name
Recognise one or two words in different contexts.								
Understand and use simple terminology such as book, right way up, front, back, upside down.								
Understand that print goes from left to right including return sweep.								
Understand that the left page comes before the right. *NB print must be on both pages when assessing this.*								
Know that print (not the picture) tells the story.								
Know that there are letters, and clusters of letters called words.								
Understand that there are first letters and last letters in words.								
Match one to one.								

Figure 2.3 Early concepts about print: group assessment record
(see Appendix for photocopiable proforma)

section two what the reading process involves

Teaching print concepts

Teaching print concepts will begin in Nursery but will be more systematic once children reach their Reception year. Ideally, children should have all print concepts in place by the end of Term 2 of Year R. A typical term by term approach for Reception would look something like this:

Term 1	Term 2	Term 3
Whole class teaching (Revision)	**Whole class teaching** Group Shared Reading	**Guided Reading**
Print concepts • Understand and use simple terminology such as: book, right way up, front, back, upside down. • Understand that print goes from left to right. • Understand that the left page comes before the right. • Know that print (not the picture) tells the story.	Print concepts • Understand and use simple terminology such as: book, right way up, front, back, upside down. • Understand that print goes from left to right. • Understand that the left page comes before the right. • Know that print (not the picture) tells the story. • Know that there are letters, and clusters of letters called words. • Understand that there are first letters and last letters in words. • Match one to one. • Link sounds to letters of the alphabet.	Examples of early Book Bands/reading targets • Cross check meaning with visual information, initial letter sound. • Predict from pictures to solve new words. • Use repeated language patterns to decode words or phrases. • Read, on the run, a small number of high frequency words - regular and irregular. • Use phonetic knowledge to decode regular words (CV and CVC). • Read without finger pointing most of the time.

Big books are ideal to demonstrate the concepts systematically. Although this will often be done in small groups, it can also be incorporated into units of work during whole class sessions. Working through a big book text in this way over several sessions will include retelling it using visuals, using role play to secure understanding, and generating ideas for writing.

Teaching one to one correspondence

The most difficult print concepts for children to grasp are:
- letters and clusters of letters called words
- first and last letters in words
- one to one correspondence.

section two

Letters and words

Distinguishing between letters and clusters of letters called words can be confusing for many children. It is very important that teachers articulate the difference by demonstrating clearly how words can be made up of letters. Before this can happen, children need to understand the difference between pictures and words making what, for some children, is an abstract concept into an everyday practice, for example:

Here is the picture of the cat, now I am going to write the word.

Let's count the letters in this word.

First and last letters

Understanding the general concept of 'first' and 'last' can be problematic for young children. This is also true when it comes to first and last letters. Again it is vital that teachers demonstrate this:

Let's count the letters in this word. Which is the first letter? Which is the last, the one right at the end?

The concept of first and last can be reinforced outside direct reading instruction in the context of everyday classroom life, such as lining up.

One to one correspondence

However, perhaps the most challenging of all print concepts to teach is one to one correspondence. Many children in the very early stages of reading find it difficult to understand that each word they say (read) is represented on the page by a group of letters.

Once one to one is established, pupils should be able to point to each word, regardless of its shape or size, as they read. For example:

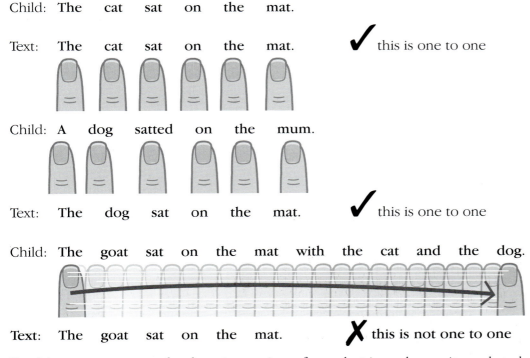

Teaching one to one can be done in a variety of ways but in each case it needs to be clearly demonstrated by the teacher. An effective method is to use a sentence strip from a known text. The teacher will point to each word while reading and then get children to try themselves.

The sentence strip can then be cut up word by word and reassembled initially by the teacher then by the pupils.

section two what the reading process involves

The children can then form 'human sentences' each holding one word as the sentence is read left to right. It is essential that the sentence is then re-read in context.

Key prompts to support this teaching might be:

What is the longest word?

What is the shortest word?

Let's count the letters in our long word.

Let's count the letters in our short word.

Let's count the words in our sentence. How many have we got?

Let's point to the words one at a time.

The concept of one to one correspondence can be taught in a range of contexts throughout the school day. For example, when lining up, when writing captions or names for displays, during shared writing sessions or during other curriculum areas, such as music.

When one to one correspondence is consistently in place, it is vital that the child no longer points at each word. By the end of Band 2, children should not be finger pointing at words.

Recommended Teaching Approaches
Vignette Year R *Teaching print concepts*

When early print concepts are included as part of a unit of work, the teaching and learning can have greater impact. This Reception teacher introduced print concepts in the context of making a class book based on *Cat on the Mat* by Brian Wildsmith, where the theme of the story is largely carried by the images. With the children gathered on the carpet area the teacher read the story as written, without interruption. This enabled the children to become familiar with the literal meaning and the animals central to it. A few children noticed that as the book progressed the animals got bigger in size and in order for all children to access this concept, the teacher retold the story using visuals to emphasise what was happening. He embellished the story adding vocabulary to support this. He also used varying tones of voice, becoming louder and more laboured by the time the elephant had arrived.

In the following session, the teacher decided to tackle the crucial theme of the invasion of personal space/territory through the use of drama. He read the story through once more then selected children to take on roles as the animals. The remainder formed an oblong shape by sitting on the carpet in order to represent the mat. The teacher retold the story, with embellishments, emphasising the fact that the space on the mat was decreasing while the annoyance of the cat was increasing. This technique enabled children to respond to questions such as: *How was the cat feeling? How do you feel when you get squashed?*

In the third session, the teacher planned to move into constructing sentences based on the story, to demonstrate the connection between print and the name of the animal. He showed the children the picture of the elephant, stressing that it is the picture that tells us which animal is on the mat. He then showed the children a sentence strip which read: 'The elephant sat on

section two

the mat' explaining that these are the words that tell us which animal is on the mat. He cut up the strip into individual words, mixed them up and talked through reassembling them to make the sentence, pointing one to one. The teacher then explained to the children that they were going to make a book using different animals. He displayed pictures of animals on the flip chart and then chose the pig and stuck the picture in the blank class book he had prepared earlier. The children orally rehearsed the sentence 'The pig sat on the mat.' several times before the teacher demonstrated writing the sentence under the picture. During this demonstration the teacher also focused on taught letter sounds in order to support transcription. He made a phoneme frame on the flipchart and the children were able to process the word 'pig'.

p	i	g

The children were then asked to select another animal and the process was repeated.

In the fourth and final session, the teacher re-read the sentences in the class book and asked for further suggestions from the children of different animals coming to sit on the mat to complete the text. The children then drew pictures to go with the words in the class book. When it was assembled, the teacher read the whole book to the class and it was put in the book area for the children to choose to read independently.

Key question

What are the most successful approaches you and your colleagues have found for teaching print concepts progressively?

It might be worth noting these as part of your policy documentation.

Teaching meaning

Children need to understand that what they read should make sense - that it should have meaning. Very young children will often pick up a book and, using the pictures, tell their own oral version of the story. This may bear no resemblance at all to what is written on the page. What they are doing is actually making meaning from the pictorial text.

Meaning is the most important source of information as it drives the reading process as a whole. When meaning is not sustained children find difficulty in decoding and understanding what is being read. In the early stages of reading development children take meaning from the pictures or illustrations in a text. At this level, pictures will support the words with no room for ambiguity or confusion.

The dog is here.	

As children develop as readers, they will begin to take meaning from the context of what they are reading. Good readers 'demand' sense.

Given the heavy emphasis on developing phonics in current practice, children have become over-reliant on using sounds (phonemes) within the words they encounter on the page. Because of this, meaning can often be neglected. However, good teaching encourages children to respond actively to the 'meaningfulness' of what they are reading and it is therefore very important for teachers to demonstrate the use of meaning when attempting unfamiliar words.

section two what the reading process involves

Recommended Teaching Approaches
Vignette Year R *Using meaning cues*

This Reception teacher wanted to model the process of tackling unfamiliar words, for example, the word 'bath' in this extract from *Where are the toys?*:

Pointing to the word 'bath', the teacher said:

I am stuck on this word. I need to find what would make sense to the story. I know, I'll look at the picture and see if that will help.

She prompted the children by offering alternatives, asking:

Would 'bed' make sense?

The children decided it wouldn't so she asked:

Why not?

And the children replied:

Because there is no bed in the picture.

Once the children began to realise that their reading should make sense, the teacher was able to prompt them to draw on other sources of information, particularly at this early stage, the pictures to support the decoding.

Teaching structure - grammar

Grammar is often tackled successfully when teaching writing, but it also needs to be systematically taught in the context of reading, demonstrating grammatical structures and how they can be used to help children attempt to read unfamiliar words. However, grammar should always be taught in the context of reading for meaning - not as a separate 'exercise'.

Oral language

It is important that children know how language is constructed in text - how it is written on the page. Sometimes children's oral language structures will differ markedly from the written word. While children are learning language they often experiment with grammatical constructions, like the past tense, for example. Cleverly noticing that some verbs use 'ed' endings in the past tense (known as regular verbs), children often over generalise and add 'ed' to irregular verbs, for example, 'runned' instead of 'ran' and 'taked' instead of 'took'. These are not strictly errors, just part of the process of getting to grips with complex English verb forms, but they need to be explained as part of discussions about spoken and written language.

Sentence structure

Texts designed for the early stages of reading will often use repeated sentence structures with just the noun changing at the end of the sentence. Children need to be made aware of how the patterns work. Initially they will learn to latch on to these structures as they are repeated on each page, for example:

section two

Here is a monkey.
Here is a lion.
Here is a giraffe.
Here is a crocodile.

As children progress, the language structures they encounter may vary, albeit only slightly at first:

The monkey went away.
The giraffe went away.
Away went the crocodile.
Away went the lion.

As texts become more complex, the structures become more variable so children need to learn the different ways that sentences can be constructed. This will be done in the context of the books selected by the teacher to highlight particular language structures.

If children are to progress as readers, other aspects of grammar need to be addressed. For example, the use of pronouns: recognising that John/he/him are all referring to the same person.

Grammar is closely linked to meaning, and is therefore a powerful source of information which helps to identify unfamiliar words. In the example above: *Here is a monkey, Here is a lion etc*, 'here is a' forms a repeated pattern or structure. Along with this, the pictures of the various animals in the text will support the process of identifying the nouns and so constructing the meaning. In this instance, meaning and sentence structure are the most useful information for word identification, not a phoneme by phoneme approach to blend words.

> *In years 1 and 2 the programmes of study for reading stress the importance of children:* **national curriculum**
> *'checking that the text makes sense to them as they read and correcting inaccurate reading'.*
> (DfE, 2014: 20 and 28)

Teaching structure - punctuation

The use of punctuation is clearly important in supporting the construction of meaning. At its most basic it is how we separate sentences in the written form. Punctuation at this level primarily consists of capital letters and full stops. From an early age children need to learn how to 'read' the punctuation they encounter, for example to learn that when they come to a full stop they should pause.

Recommended Teaching Approaches
Vignette Year R *Teaching grammatical structure and punctuation*

Prompting children to use structure at the point of error to help children learn to use grammatical cues when approaching unfamiliar words, this Reception teacher began with a common error. She had prepared the sentence: *John ran down the road* in enlarged print but as she showed it to the children, she read it as: *John runned down the road*. She wanted the children to notice when a sentence doesn't sound right, so she modelled:

> *I don't think 'runned' sounds right. I need to think about how it is written in a story.*
> *I know, we can't say 'runned' we have to say 'ran'.*

To consolidate recognition of common errors with irregular verbs like *runned/ran, sawed/saw, taked/took*, the teacher made 'sound right cards' for the children to sort out. The children began to hear the irregularities and remove them from their reading.

In focusing on punctuation, the teacher demonstrated how the voice should sound. She prepared these sentences in enlarged print:

section two what the reading process involves

> '**Sit down,' said the teacher.** Which she read with a calm voice to signal that it just means 'Sit down everyone.'
>
> '**Sit down! said the teacher.** Read with a cross voice suggesting: 'Sit down right this minute.'
>
> '**Sit down?' said the teacher.** With a bewildered voice and looking around her for a chair, indicating: 'Do you really want me to sit down?
>
> After she had read each sentence she asked the children:
>
> *Does that sound right?*
>
> *Do we say it like that in books?*
>
> *How should our voice sound when we read an exclamation mark?*
>
> *How should it sound when we read a question mark?*
>
> To get the children themselves involved in looking at sentence structure and punctuation, on separate large cards she prepared the sentence: "I am up," said the pig.
>
> | " | I | am | up | , | " | said | the | pig | . |
>
> She gave different children the individual cards and asked the rest of the class to help them make the sentence read correctly with the punctuation in the right place. She found that using 'human sentences' like this helped the children get to grips with sentence structure and punctuation quite quickly, particularly in identifying speech marks where confusion can arise about who is speaking and when a speaker changes.

Key question

How have you and your colleagues successfully taught grammatical structure and punctuation in years R, 1 and 2?

It might be worth noting these as part of your policy documentation.

Teaching visual information

Visual information is the PRINT. It consists of the letters and words actually written on the page. Images, graphics or decorated page borders are classed as pictorial, not visual sources of information. Visual information falls into two main categories:

- phonological awareness
- graphic knowledge.

Both are vital in supporting children to decode unfamiliar words.

Teaching phonics

In the very early stages of reading, children need to develop sound discrimination so that they are able to distinguish between familiar sounds within their environment. Initially, they need to be able to separate quite distinctive sounds. As more formal instruction begins, children need to be aware of the sounds (phonemes) represented by the letters in the alphabet, so that they are able to use them to blend for reading. They need to know that there are 26 letters and 44 phonemes which are represented by letters or combinations of letters.

section two

Consonant phonemes		Vowel phonemes	
Sound	*Examples*	**Sound**	*Examples*
/b/	Bat	/a/	ant
/k/ (c)	Cat	/e/	egg
/d/	dog	/i/	in
/f/	fan	/o/	on
/g/	go	/u/	up
/h/	hen	/ai/	rain
/j/	jet	/ar/	farm
/l/	leg	/ee/	feet
/m/	map	/er/	kerb
/n/	net	/igh/	night
/p/	pen	/oa/	boat
/kw/ (qu)	queen	/oi/	coin
/r/	rat	/oo/	boot
/s/	sun	/oo/	look
/t/	tap	/or/	for
/v/	van	/ou/	out
/w/	wig	/ow/	cow
/y/	yes	/ur/	hurt
/z/	zip	/air/	fair
/sh/	shop	/ear/	dear
/ch/	chip		
/th/	thin		
/th/	then		
/ng/	ring		
/zh/	vision		

Adapted from the Primary National Strategy *Letters and Sounds: Notes of Guidance for Practitioners and Teachers* (DfES, 2007)

There are different ways of teaching phonics: synthetic and analytic. These methods require different approaches to decoding unfamiliar words using visual information:

Synthetic phonics refers to an approach in which the sounds identified with letters are learned in isolation and blended together, for example, a synthetic approach to reading 'cat' would require children to decode the word phoneme by phoneme 'c-a-t'.

Analytic phonics refers to an approach where the sounds associated with letters are not pronounced in isolation but children identify phonic elements for words which each contain a similar element, either at the start of the word (before the first vowel) - onset - or in the later part of the word - rime. So to read the word 'cat' would require children to recognise the rime 'at' and then add the onset 'c'.

Research strongly indicates that using both approaches in combination is more effective than using either on its own (Juel and Minden-Cupp, 2001).

The National Curriculum in England and Wales (DfE, 2014) requires that synthetic phonics be used in the first instance. However, as children's reading vocabulary increases and becomes more varied and complex, they are likely to use both synthetic and analytic approaches.

section two what the reading process involves

In the initial stages, the discrimination of distinctive sounds can be taught through speaking and listening activities including music. By developing the ability to distinguish between sounds, children will improve their phonological awareness. This can also be done by working on rhymes and alliteration. As children move into more formal instruction, most phonics programmes introduce the letters **s, a, t, p, i, n**. These sounds give children the opportunity to blend many phonically regular words quickly adopting a phoneme by phoneme approach. At this stage children will learn further phonemes and develop an understanding of phoneme-grapheme correspondences.

Children will then move on to learn further phoneme/grapheme correspondences, including different ways of making the vowel sounds, such as ie (as in *lie*), i-e (as in *side*) and igh (as in *high*). They will recognise a range of digraphs (two letters making one sound), trigraphs (three letters making one sound) and adjacent consonants and become familiar with phonic irregularities, however, much of this learning can be made easier by an analytic approach particularly appealing to children's capacity to use analogy.

national curriculum

In year 1 pupils should be taught to:
- *respond speedily with the correct sound to graphemes (letters or groups of letters) for all 40+ phonemes, including, where applicable, alternative sounds for graphemes*
- *read accurately by blending sounds in unfamiliar words containing GPCs that have been taught*
- *read common exception words, noting unusual correspondences between spelling and sound and where these occur in the word*
- *read words containing taught GPCs and -s, -es, -ing, -ed, -er and -est endings*
- *read other words of more than one syllable that contain taught GPCs*
- *read words with contractions, e.g. I'm, I'll, we'll, and understand that the apostrophe represents the omitted letter(s).* (DfE, 2014: 19)

It is important that phonics sessions happen every day. They should be multi-sensory, pacey and lively. Sessions should be short (a maximum of 20 minutes) and, although discrete, should provide opportunities for the teacher to demonstrate the application of skills allowing children to practise segmenting and blending. This should be done during the phonics lesson itself but can also be developed in the context of Guided and Shared Reading sessions.

Phonics teaching also requires the technical skill of enunciation. Phonemes should be articulated clearly and precisely as many errors spring from incorrect pronunciation. Although many sounds, particularly vowel sounds, can vary slightly according to accent, they are generally consistent within the speech of an individual and recognisable by others who may pronounce them differently.

However, it is particularly important for teachers to be sensitive to regional accents and to be aware of the danger of 'mishearing' words (e.g. 'brine' for 'brain' in London). Teachers should avoid suggesting that there is one 'received' way of pronouncing words.

The terminology of phonics

Children should learn the correct terminology. It is important that both teachers and pupils have a common understanding of definitions and what they mean.

section two

Terminology	Definition
Phoneme	The smallest unit of sound in a word.
Grapheme	Letter(s) representing a phoneme.
Digraph	Two letters that represent one phoneme. A consonant digraph contains two consonants: sh ck th ll A vowel digraph contains at least one vowel: ai ee ar oy
Split digraph	A digraph in which the two letters are not adjacent: m <u>a</u> k <u>e</u>
Trigraph	Three letters that represent one phoneme: igh dge
Blending	Recognising the letter sounds in a written word, for example c-u-p and merging or synthesising them in the order in which they are written to pronounce the word 'cup'.
Oral blending	Hearing a series of spoken sounds and merging them together to make a spoken word - no letters are used. For example, when a teacher calls out 'b-u-s', the children say 'bus'. This skill is usually taught before blending and reading printed words.
Segmenting	Identifying the individual phonemes in a spoken word (e.g. h-i-m) and writing down or manipulating letters for each phoneme to form the word 'him'.

Teaching should be done in whole class or group sessions which follow the lesson sequence:
- revisit/review
- teach
- practise
- apply
- independent practice.

Letters and Sounds (DfES, 2007) gives a progressive programme of phonics teaching. Available on: https://www.gov.uk/government/uploads/system/uploads/attachment_data/file/190599/Letters_and_Sounds_-_DFES-00281-2007.pdf).

Recommended Teaching Approaches
Graphic information

Even at the early stages of reading development, a sizeable number of the words children encounter will not necessarily be phonically regular. This includes texts which have been written to accompany specific phonics programmes. Children will need, therefore, to draw on other forms of visual information. Graphic information comprises all other types of visual information that does not fall under the phonics umbrella. It is vital knowledge which children need in order to work out unfamiliar words. Graphic information allows children to read whole words (high frequency), chunks of words including simple prefixes such as un, pre and inflectional

section two what the reading process involves

endings such as ing, ed. It also allows them to use their knowledge of parts of words to build other words (onset and rime) such as ight - right, bright, tight etc.

It is important in the early stages that children are taught simple graphic information particularly high frequency words. They need to learn a bank of words that arise frequently in texts and these should be learnt as graphic information so they can be read 'on the run'. Children should not be 'sounding out' these words whether they are phonically regular or not. By definition, as they are frequently encountered in texts, if children stop to blend them, the fluency of the reading will be affected and meaning may be lost.

High frequency words can be taught through whole class teaching or in Guided Reading sessions. An effective way of teaching high frequency words is by using magnetic letters, boards and word cards. The teacher uses the cards and magnetic letters in tandem, holding up the card first so the children can read the word. They then use the magnetic letters to form the word.

s a i d   **said**

Magnetic letters   *Word card*

The teacher can then mix the letters up and ask the children to re-assemble the word, saying it as they do so.

a i s d

At all times, the children should be reminded to check the magnetic letters against the high frequency word card.

Then, and very importantly, they should find the word in the book they are working on and read it in context.

It is important that only two or three words are taught in any one session and each word worked on one at a time. Words that are easily confused should not be taught together.

Alongside high frequency words, other types of graphic information are also important for the early reader. This is particularly so of onset and rime. This can be taught, again in the context of the book, by highlighting and learning the rimes and then building words by adding the onsets.

Simple onsets and rimes are:

   rime *in* onsets p*in* b*in* t*in*
   rime *at* onsets h*at* s*at* b*at*

Slightly more complex are:

   rime *ain* onsets tr*ain* br*ain* g*ain*
   rime *ight* onsets f*ight* l*ight* br*ight*

Figure 2.4 gives examples of rimes that make nearly five hundred words.

section two

-ack	-ame	-ate	-ice	-in	-ock	-ug
-ain	-an	-aw	-ick	-ing	-oke	-ump
-ake	-ap	-ay	-ide	-ink	-op	-unk
-ale	-ash	-eat	-ite	-ip	-ore	
-all	-at	-est	-ill	-ir	-uck	

Figure 2.4 Rimes that make nearly 500 words

As children develop further as readers, other types of graphic information need to be learnt. Information about prefixes and suffixes (which also supports meaning and structure), syllabification and compound words are very helpful in solving words visually.

> *In year 2, pupils should be taught to:*
> - read accurately by blending the sounds in words that contain the graphemes taught so far, especially recognising alternative sounds for graphemes
> - read accurately words of two or more syllables that contain the same GPCs as above
> - read words containing common suffixes
> - read further common exception words, noting unusual correspondence between spelling and sound and where these occur in the word
> - read most words quickly and accurately when they have been frequently encountered without overt sounding and blending (DfE, 2014: 25)
>
> **national curriculum**

Early progression in sources of information

The early progression of sources of information would gradually enable children to use more sophisticated meaning, structure and visual cues (see Figure 2.5) and also enable them to begin to orchestrate all three sources at once. This would mirror the increasing difficulty of texts described in Section One (see pages 22-23).

section two what the reading process involves

	Book Band 1	**Book Band 2**	**Book Band 3**	**Book Band 4**
Meaning	Children use pictures to work out and predict unfamiliar words, for example, *'I am laughing.'*	Children use pictures to work out and predict unfamiliar words, for example, *"I am asleep," said the Pig.*	Children use pictures to work out new words. They begin to use the context of the story, for example, *'Dad and Rachel and Lucky went home.'*	Children use pictures to work out new words. They begin to use the context of the story, for example, *'Baby bear went into the forest.'*
Structure *(grammar)*	Children recognise and read the repeated pattern within texts, for example, *'I am laughing.' 'I am crying.'*	Children recognise and read two and three word phrases that have repeated patterns throughout. For example, *'I am up'*, and note when the pattern is not repeated, for example, *'I am up... said the pig.' 'I am up... said the cow.' 'I am asleep said the pig.'*	Children predict and solve words using grammatical structure, for example, *'Come here, Lucky.'*	Children predict and solve words using grammatical structure, for example, *'Spot, called Sam.'*
Structure *(punctuation)*		Children use capital letters and full stops when reading.	Children use full stops, exclamation marks and speech marks when reading.	Children use a range of punctuation while reading, for example, full stops, exclamation marks, speech marks and question marks.
Visual *(graphophonic)*	Children blend phonemes to decode simple VC and CVC words. For example, *h-a-t; b-a-g*.	Children read CVC words such as *b oa t sh o p*. They should run the sounds together.	Children use phonics to read words with adjacent consonants. For example, *b e st cl a p j u mp*.	Children use knowledge of long vowel phonemes and adjacent consonants to blend longer, unfamiliar words. For example, *t ea ch er*.
Visual *(graphic)*	Children learn some high frequency words that they can locate in text.	Children learn more high frequency words that they can locate in text.	Children learn a broader range of high frequency words that they can read on the run. Children read familiar words noting clusters of letters, for example, *look, book, took, cat, sat, mat*.	Children learn a broader range of high frequency words that they can read on the run. Children look beyond the initial letter of the word by demonstrating: • inflectional endings, for example, *climb/climbing, look/looked* • analogy, for example, *make, take, wake*.

Left: *Figure 2.5 Early progression in sources of information for word identification*

Teaching reading strategies

Reading strategies are used to pick up, process and put together the information (meaning, structure, visual) that children have acquired. What children need to be able to do ultimately is to orchestrate all sources of information. Teaching reading strategies must be systematic and explicit and can be most effectively carried out during Guided Reading sessions. Teaching reading strategies means building a processing system which is self-extending so that competent readers will have a range of reading strategies to call upon in order read independently.

Underpinning the whole reading process is children's ability to:

- self-monitor
- cross check
- re-read
- search for more information
- orchestrate all sources of information
- read on
- self-correct.

The child's use of the cueing systems has been compared to a conductor directing an orchestra. The orchestra metaphor emphasises the harmony achieved when all systems blend together. (Mallett, 2005:1)

Learning how to read is fundamentally a task of learning how to orchestrate knowledge in a skilful manner. (Bussis et al., 1985:113)

Strategies tend to be hierarchical and in the early stages children will need to self-monitor and cross check. As children develop as readers, they acquire the ability to read on, re-read and search for more information in order to self-correct. Self-monitoring is crucial to developing independence (see Figure 2.6). It is not possible for children to search for more information and self-correct if they are not aware that they have made an error in the first place. Self-monitoring for meaning and structure are crucial. Children need to determine whether their reading makes sense and sounds right. The process in Figure 2.6 is not necessarily sequential and staged but may be iterative, with readers checking back and forward as they read.

Self-monitoring leading to self-correction
(picking up, working on, putting together)

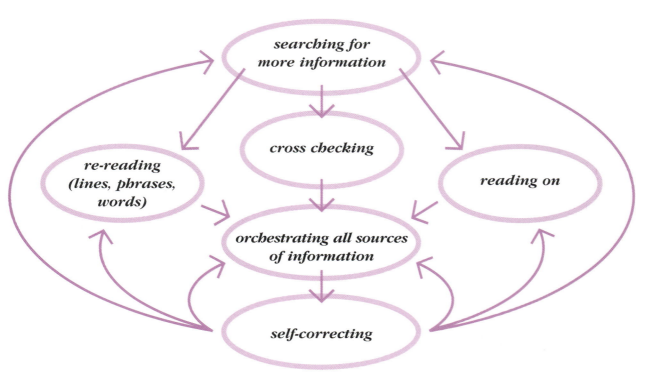

Figure 2.6 Self-monitoring leading to self-correction (drawn from Clay, 2008: 108-9)

section two what the reading process involves

Recommended Teaching Approaches
Vignette Year R *Cross checking, self-monitoring and self-correcting*

Children will take some time to learn to use all reading strategies independently. Although cross checking with the picture is a very early strategy that will not support independence much after the very early stages (Book Band 2) through use of this strategy, children can be encouraged to self-monitor and although they may not be able to search for further information in order to self-correct, the first step is to recognise that an error has been made.

This Reception teacher used a Guided Reading session to help the group develop the ability to cross-check using the picture. In this text, the unfamiliar word is 'running'. She covered the word with a sticky note then asked them to look at the picture: *Look at the picture. What would make sense?*

The children responded:

Happy

So the teacher replied:

Well 'happy' would make sense. If it was 'happy' what phoneme would you hear at the beginning of the word?

Chorus of children:

H.

Revealing the initial letters, the teacher explained:

We don't have a 'h'. There is a 'r' so what would make sense and look right at the beginning of the word?

A few children were able to supply: running! which the teacher confirmed, going on to emphasise the link between the picture and the words:

Yes. You must look at the picture first to see what would make sense and then look at the beginning of the word to check that you have the correct phoneme.

In order to develop further strategies, in Shared Reading she demonstrated self-monitoring and self-correcting. Using sentence strips from the text, she read a sentence, making deliberate errors. To make the process explicit she stopped, then returned to the sentence and read correctly:

My reading didn't make sense so I had to stop and try and fix it up.

She then read a few more, using the same process so that the children could see how she was self-monitoring. In order to practise and consolidate this strategy, in Guided Reading sessions the teacher encouraged the children to listen to their own reading and stop when they lost the meaning or the structure, giving support to help them self-correct.

Figure 2.7 indicates possible prompts and key teaching points for developing reading strategies.

Right: Figure 2.7 Prompts for teaching reading strategies

section two

Strategy	Prompt	Key teaching points
Self-monitoring	*Listen to your reading. Does it make sense?* *If your reading doesn't make sense then stop.*	Ask children to listen to their own reading and check for meaning. Demonstrate this by: • reading sentences from the texts, making deliberate errors and stopping, saying: *That didn't make sense so I have to stop.* • encouraging the children to listen and monitor the teacher's reading and when deliberate mistakes are made, saying where the error occurred.
Cross checking	*How else can you check?* *If it was... what letter would you see at the beginning?* *What would make sense and look right?*	Ask children to use the picture to attempt the word (meaning) and to check their attempt by looking at the initial letter (visual information). Demonstrate this by: • using sticky notes to cover tricky words and asking children to say what they think might fit (make sense) • asking children to check their predictions by looking at the initial letter.
Re-reading	*Go back and read it again.* *Read that part and find what would fit.*	Ask children to go back and re-read (usually to the beginning of the sentence) to find what would make sense, sound right and look right. Demonstrate this by: • using sentence strips from the text, making a deliberate mistake and re-reading to find what would make sense.
Searching for more information	*Do you know another word like that?* *What do you know that might help?*	Ask children to listen to their own reading and check for meaning. Demonstrate this by: • reading sentences from the texts, making deliberate errors and stopping then saying: *That didn't make sense so I have to stop and look for more clues.* • reading sentences from the texts, making deliberate errors and stopping then saying: *That didn't make sense so I have to stop to see if that is how we say it in books and I have to look closely at the word.*
Orchestrating all sources of information	*What would look right, sound right and make sense?* *What's wrong?*	Ask children to go back and re-read (usually to the beginning of the sentence) to find what would make sense, sound right and look right. Demonstrate this by: • using sentence strips from the text making deliberate mistakes and re-reading to find what would make sense, sound right and look right • emphasising that all three sources of information need to be checked.
Reading on	*Leave that word and read to the end.* *Read the sentence then go back and check.*	Ask children to leave the word they are stuck on and read to the end of the sentence to see if they can find what would make sense. Demonstrate this by: • using sentence strips from the text, stopping at a tricky word and reading to the end of the sentence, returning to the tricky word and making a meaningful substitution.
Self-correcting	*You made a mistake. Can you find it?* *Try that again.*	Ask children to listen to their own reading and check for meaning. Demonstrate this by: • reading sentences from the texts, making deliberate errors and stopping then saying: *That didn't make sense so I have to stop. Now I have to fix it up by thinking what would sound right and look right.*

section two what the reading process involves

Teaching reading behaviours

Alongside sources of information and strategies, children need to develop reading behaviours. Some of these are:

- reading English print from left to right
- reading fluently without finger pointing
- reading longer phrases and more complex sentences with expression
- reading silently most of the time.

In the early stages, reading behaviours are based on the early concepts about print (see page 37) but as children develop as readers other behaviours need to be taught. Perhaps the most important one is that of fluency and phrasing. Fluent reading is key to maintaining meaning and, of course, developing comprehension. As children develop further as readers the ability to read longer texts - reading stamina - is important as is the skill of reading silently. Children do not acquire reading behaviours without direct instruction; as with early print concepts, they need to be systematically taught. In addition to this, children need to hear a range of texts read aloud in order to internalise how fluent and phrased reading should sound.

Recommended Teaching Approaches
Vignette *Developing fluency and phrasing*

One of the most crucial reading behaviours is that of fluency, phrasing and expression. In the early stages, two or three word phrases such as 'said mum', 'said the boy', 'off we go!' would be highlighted but the length of the phrases will be built up over time. When working on fluency and phrasing, children should not be finger pointing.

In Shared Reading this Reception teacher began by reading the text without showing it to the children

"Little brown bear,
Little brown bear,
Please will you help me?"
Said the little brown mouse.

She asked the class:

Pretend you are little brown mouse and you want little brown bear to play with you. How would you say those words?

Shane remembered one sentence and said, with some expression:

Please will you help me?

The teacher replied:

Very good - you sound like you really want little brown bear to help you.

She then put the book on the stand, and putting thumb and forefinger around the sentence, asked Shane to read the words on the page:

Now see if you can read the words like that.

Shane read from the book:

Please will you help me?

section two

> The teacher then returned to the top of the page, inviting the class to read the words with expression.
>
> Focusing on reading for fluency meant that at times the teacher used a variety of prompts:
> *Make your reading sound like a story.*
> *How do you think xxx might have said those words?*
> *Keep the story going.*
> *Run those words together.*

Children who experience difficulty with reading

No matter what instruction children receive, there will always be some who find the process of reading difficult. These pupils often have key characteristics in common, but it is necessary, through rigorous assessment, to unpick exactly what is 'getting in the way' for individual children.

Lower attaining readers:

- tend not to use meaning as a source of information
- tend to have :
  - poor word level skills
  - poor phonological awareness
  - difficulty with recall of high frequency words
- tend to be over reliant on being 'told' words rather than having strategies to problem solve
- often read slowly giving the same weight to each word
- often read without fluency or expression
- often finger point
- often have limited vocabulary
- tend to lack real or imagined experiences that they can bring to a text
- tend to have poor grammatical skills
- are often over reliant on one source of information - usually visual
- are often over reliant on one strategy - usually 'sounding out'.

Quality whole class teaching, with no intervention, does not enable children with literacy difficulties to catch up. Schools may use commercial programmes to support children who experience difficulty with reading and often lower attaining pupils receive intervention in small groups with a Teaching Assistant, rather than extra support from the class teacher.

What works successfully for most children who struggle is when:

- work on phonological skills for reading is embedded within a range of contexts which have meaning as the priority
- comprehension skills are directly targeted
- children's self-esteem is developed alongside their reading
- reading is carefully modelled by the teacher
- reading partners are available and are given appropriate training and support
- interventions do not last longer than one term
- expectations are high.

Although intervention programmes are absolutely vital to ensure accelerated learning, the role of the class teacher is crucial to ensure informed and continuing monitoring of progress.

section two what the reading process involves

Recommended Teaching Approaches
Supporting children who are experiencing difficulties with reading

Check your own actions:

>Am I making the wrong assumptions about what the child can/can't do?
>Am I taking strengths and weaknesses into account?
>Am I encouraging dependence or independence?

Check your records of progress:

>What difficulties have I noted?
>What evidence is there of successful learning or failure?

Observe the child's behaviour:

>Why might s/he be experiencing difficulties with some aspects of reading?
>Ask other adults who know the child about the perceived difficulties. Can you identify anything that is interfering with progress?

Work from the known

Make sure the reader knows what the story is about before reading.

Have realistic expectations

Ask children to do everything they can do but don't expect them to do what they can't.

Encourage and support independence

When the child is 'stuck' on a word, transfer the task to the reader, asking:

>What do you know that starts with that letter?
>Read the sentence again and get your mouth ready.
>Why did you stop?
>What did you notice?

Avoid confusion:

>Only do what is needed now - not what might help in the future.
>Don't teach similar shaped letters or similar looking words together.

Focus on essentials:

>Be sure what the most important teaching points are.
>Ignore other inadequacies.

Consolidate learning:

>Every new thing learned should be revised in several other activities.

Work for fluency:

>When the reading is phrased like spoken language and the response is fluent, this suggests that the reader can read for meaning.
>
>(adapted from Clay, 2008: 180-182)

See Appendix for photocopiable proforma to help identify reading difficulties and plan for intervention.

section three comprehension

Comprehension

> Good comprehension draws from linguistic knowledge (in particular of vocabulary and grammar) and on knowledge of the world. Comprehension skills develop through pupils' experience of high-quality discussion with the teacher, as well as from reading and discussing a range of stories, poems and non-fiction. (DfE, 2014:14)
>
> **national curriculum**

Moving to deeper understanding

Comprehension, or understanding, is an active process occurring before, during and after reading. It requires the use of a range of strategies in order to understand, on all levels, what the author is saying. Fluent and experienced readers have the ability to check continually that they have understood what they are reading.

There have been many attempts to define reading comprehension. Pardo (2004) sees it as:

> A process in which readers construct meaning by interacting with text through the combination of prior knowledge and previous experience, information in the text and the stance the reader takes in relationship to the text (p. 272).

But perhaps the clearest is Frank Smith's foundational (1978) definition:

> Prediction is asking questions - and comprehension is getting these questions answered. (p. 66)

Comprehension involves not just getting meaning out of the text:

> Comprehension is concerned as much with what the reader brings to the text as it is with what the reader gets out of the text. (Morrison, 1994: 32)

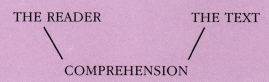

There are key elements which support children in taking meaning from texts related to:

- structural features
- vocabulary
- prior knowledge or experience
- grammatical skills.

Structural features of text

The structural layout of the text is important to the way it is read. In some cases text structure can enhance the meaning or add to the emphasis or mood, for example, a recipe, information leaflet or picturebook uses layout and illustration specifically to aid understanding. Children need to learn how to interpret layout as they learn to read. In narrative texts designed for early reading instruction, Book Bands 1 and 2 in particular, the features of the text are predictable: the layout of the words is consistent and they are always on the same part of the page. As texts become more complex, features such as the vocabulary, illustrations, text layout including dialogue, typography and interactive elements such as fold-out pages are not always as predictable and can sometimes prevent children taking meaning from what they read. Similarly, with non-fiction texts, the features such as captions, labels, subtitles and charts make navigation more challenging.

When working with more complex or detailed texts, including picturebooks or information texts, teachers need to draw children's attention to the specific features which may challenge them in terms of reading comprehension.

section three comprehension

Vocabulary

In order to fully understand what they read, pupils need to develop a broad and rich vocabulary and it is important that teachers deal with any misconceptions without making assumptions about what may or may not be within the children's lexicon. For example in the Band 1 text *Dressing Up* (Randall *et al.* 1996: 10) there is a page which says: 'I am a pirate' with a picture of a pirate opposite. If children don't actually know what a pirate is they will find it impossible to predict and take meaning from the word 'pirate', which means that discussing unfamiliar vocabulary and rehearsing it is very important.

As vocabulary becomes more challenging, it can prevent children taking meaning from what is being read. Teachers need to explore new words but it is not enough to just offer definitions. The use of drama, pictorial support and real objects is important, but it is also necessary for children to encounter these words in a range of contexts, for example, through reading other texts or accessing other forms of media, such as film (see, for example, The Literacy Shed website on http://www.literacyshed.com/).

Prior knowledge or experience

Lack of prior knowledge and understanding of the world that children bring to texts can often be problematic in making meaning. If they are going to predict and make connections, even text-to-self connections, young readers will need to have a number of real or imagined experiences on which to draw. As children get older, they may be able to bring more diverse life experiences to reading, but this is not always the case.

Role play and drama techniques are crucial in providing children with the experiences they need. The construction of images through drama techniques such as 'tableaux', providing opportunities for children to question and clarify through working with a partner, hot seating (character empathy) and making connections are also important in supporting children's understanding. Choice of stimulus is crucial and often the use of multimodal texts will enable children, through visual images, to develop knowledge and opinions, thus providing further experience to bring to a text.

Grammatical skills

Grammatical knowledge plays an important role in comprehension. In developing readers this will be learnt and internalised through their oral language experiences. It is important that children know how language is constructed at sentence level (syntax), it is also important that they understand morphology - how units of meaning combine to make words. For example, the three separate units of meaning: 'in', 'come', 'ing' can be combined to make the word 'incoming'. 'Cat' and 's' (two separate units of meaning) combine to make the word 'cats'. Grammatical knowledge supports understanding particularly when children are learning English as an additional language. For example, the use of pronouns - children need to know who or what is being referred to in order to comprehend:

*Sebastian climbed the mountain. By the time **he** got to the top **he** was tired.*

They need to be able to recognise that 'Sebastian' and 'he' are the same person.

As children develop as readers, other grammatical constructions like the passive voice are important because they can change emphasis or mood and therefore meaning. Teaching grammatical constructions must always be done in the context of books children are reading and not through 'grammar exercises'.

section three

Teaching reading comprehension

As a general rule, comprehension in early reading development is usually seen as simple recall, sequencing of events or making simple predictions. Children are often prompted to look at the front cover of a text and say what they think the book might be about. There is little prediction during or indeed after reading has taken place. Often, as children develop as readers, comprehension tends to be seen as 'twenty questions on a page' many of which require children to merely retrieve information literally from the text and provide written responses often in full sentences, for example:

Question sheet	*Pupil response*
What colour is the boy's coat?	*The boy's coat is red.*
Where is the dog?	*The dog is in the garden.*

This kind of question and answer tells the teacher very little about the child's understanding of the text and does even less to develop it. In the programmes of study for reading, progression is seen both as a broadening of experience of types of text and an increasing ability to offer opinions based on the text:

> *In year 1:*
> *listening to and discussing a wide range of poems, stories and non-fiction.* (DfE, 2014: 20)
>
> *In year 2:*
> *listening to, discussing and expressing views about a wide range of poetry (including contemporary and classic), stories and non-fiction.* (ibid.: 27)

national curriculum

But in order support the full development of reading comprehension, children need to be introduced to a wider range of strategies:

- Summarising
- Predicting
- Visualising
- Questioning
- Connecting
- Inferring.

The following sections give vignette examples of teachers supporting children's learning of a range of strategies. All the ideas are easily adaptable for use with any picturebook, film clip, poem, song or story.

Summarising

Summarising allows children to gain an overall understanding of the text by recalling key events or sequencing the narrative. The following examples give suggestions for using a range of texts to teach summarising at Reception, Year 1 and Year 2.

section three comprehension

Recommended Teaching Approaches
Vignette Year R *Summarising*

As part of their literacy work, a Reception class was exploring the song 'Miss Molly had a Dolly' with a view to writing a class book to share in assembly. Prior to the session, the teacher had taught the children the song and they had revisited it several times.

With the children gathered on the carpet, the teacher showed the film clip 'Miss Molly had a Dolly' (YouTube Kidzteddy, Miss Molly) and played it through twice encouraging the children to join in. She then chose children to be the main characters giving them props such as a blanket, telephone, doctor's bag, stethoscope etc. As the teacher summarised the song, the children acted in role. This enabled them to become even more familiar with the story. At each key part of the summarising, the teaching assistant took digital photographs.

The props were then put in the outdoor area so that the children could retell the story/song independently.

During the following session, the children used print-outs of the digital photos to summarise the story to each other in pairs. Later these photos formed the prompts for sentence writing.

This could be done with any song or rhyme that has a cumulative story, for example 'The Old Lady who Swallowed a Fly' or 'Bought me a Cat'.

Vignette Year 1 *Summarising*

As part of a unit of work based on the book *Six Little Chicks* by Jez Alborough, this Year 1 teacher wanted to explore the central theme within the text with a view to getting children to write simple stories of their own. Before she could do this, the children needed to become very familiar with the text in a literal sense.

With her class gathered on the carpet, the teacher read the story through without interruption. Following the reading, she retold the story using key visuals embellishing particular sections throughout, in order to enhance the meaning and introduce new vocabulary. She then displayed the visuals on the flipchart.

The children worked in pairs, some supported by the Teaching Assistant, and chose six key visuals from the original nine the teacher had displayed. They were then asked to retell the story to each other, using the six visuals they had chosen. While the children were retelling, the teacher supported targeted pairs.

You can use any picturebook with distinct key events for summarising.

Vignette Year 2 *Summarising*

As an introduction to a two week unit of work which was to culminate in narrative writing, the Year 2 teacher introduced the children to the film clip 'The Windmill Farmer' (a short film by Joachin Baldwin available on YouTube). Following the initial showing she retold key points from the film. The teacher explained to the children that they were going to watch the film again and as they were doing so, they had to take particular notice of what happened and in what order. To support this she displayed some prompt cards on the flipchart: *What happened first? What happened after the storm? What did the farmer do after the storm? What happened at the end?*

Following the second showing, in their mixed ability pairs, the children retold the story to one another, taking turns at telling different parts. Together they selected six key points which they noted down on sticky notes and put in order. The teacher then selected several pairs to give feedback and together the class came to a consensus about the six key points to choose. These were scribed on the flipchart to form the basis of a plan for shared writing.

There are plenty of good film clips on The Literacy Shed website (http://www.literacyshed.com/), or YouTube. You just need to find one with a clear storyline.

Predicting

Predicting allows children to think about what might happen next in a story. This can take place before, during or after reading. Although children will use a range of clues such as the pictures and the written text, prediction primarily requires them to draw on prior knowledge and experience. In the following examples, teachers develop prediction using picturebooks with Reception, Year 1 and Year 2 classes.

Recommended Teaching Approaches

Vignette Year R *Predicting*

As part of her literacy work, this Reception class teacher planned for the children to make a class book based on *Rosie's Walk* by Pat Hutchins. In order for them to have a good understanding of the text, she wanted the children to make predictions based on their prior knowledge and understanding. To support this she started the lesson by displaying the front cover of the book and asking the children to look closely at the picture, prompting them to think about what they could see and who they could see.

In pairs, the children then discussed what they thought the story might be about and where it was taking place. The teacher took feedback from their discussions and scribed some predictions on the flipchart. Still using the front cover, she focused on the fox. The children discussed what they thought the fox might be going to do. During the discussion, the teacher prompted the children to give reasons for their predictions. She then read the book to the children pointing out the correct predictions as she moved through the text. She retold the story using visuals.

The children then worked in pairs, re-telling the story using the visuals as a starting point for making their own class book.

It is best to choose a book with a familiar (real or imaginary) setting or characters so that children can make predictions based on their own prior knowledge. A strong cover image is also a plus.

Vignette Year 1 *Predicting*

As part of her literacy work, this Year 1 teacher introduced *Room on the Broom* by Julia Donaldson. With the children gathered on the carpet, she displayed the front cover asking them to look closely at it and think about what the story might be about. They told her that it was about a witch. The children, in pairs, then discussed what the witch was doing, where she was going and who was going with her. This allowed the children to make predictions based on their prior knowledge drawn from other stories about witches.

The teacher then read the story to the children up to the point just before the broomstick snaps. She displayed the illustration where all the animals are on the broomstick. The children, in pairs, predicted what might happen next. The teacher generated a range of responses from them, discussing each one, at the same time getting children to explain their thinking. Slowly turning the page, she revealed that the broom snaps. The children were then able to check their predictions against what happened in the text.

section three comprehension

In the following sessions, she used one of the children's predictions to change the end of the story. This was made into a class book called 'Room on the Broom - the other story'.

It is best to choose a story that has one or two good 'cliffhangers' so that the children will be able to make predictions at different points in the narrative, for example, *Fox* by Margaret Wild.

Vignette Year 2 *Predicting*

As part of a longer unit of work on traditional tales, through a range of activities in previous sessions, this Year 2 class had become very familiar with the text *The Adventures of the Dish and the Spoon* by Mini Grey. The teacher wanted the children to write the sequel to the story. The children worked in pairs to describe the characteristics of the Dish and the Spoon and these were scribed on the flipchart and discussed further. The children were then asked to make predictions about what the characters might do next. The teacher prompted them to keep their ideas true to the traits of the characters.

During the feedback session the teacher selected some pairs to share their predictions. The children discussed what they thought would happen next. There was some debate about whether characters change, about how they act, think or feel and whether they learn from their mistakes. If the Dish and the Spoon changed, how might this change the sequel?

The children then wrote their sequels independently.

For most successful prediction, you need a book, or a narrative poem, with strong characters and with a storyline that could lead to a sequel, for example *Pumpkin Soup* by Helen Cooper or *Down by the Cool of the Pool* by Tony Mitton.

Visualising

Visualising is about children creating images in their mind's eye as they read. It is about activating children's imaginations - what they sense, particularly what they see and using their senses to 'dive into' the story using prior knowledge and experiences. As children read, they revise and refine their visualisations. Pictorial representation and drama are useful ways of getting children to make those visualisations. In the following examples, a range of texts, including poetry and film, are used to support visualisation.

Recommended Teaching Approaches

Vignette Year R *Visualising*

This Reception teacher introduced the text *The Train Ride* by June Crebbin by explaining to the children that it was about a little girl going to visit her grandma on a train and that on the journey the train would pass a lot of things. She then read the text without interruption to the children.

The teacher retold the story with an emphasis on what the train had passed during the journey. This was not done in rhyme as in the book but in a narrative style. (*Past the sheep, past the cows* etc). To support this she used visuals from the text of the sheep, cows, mare, foal, farm, tractor, geese, trees, the town, lighthouse, station.

The children then moved to the outdoor area where the teacher chose pupils to tableau the setting. She also chose two children to be the tunnel and one to be the train. As the teacher retold the story once more, 'the train' made the journey. Digital photographs were taken of each part of the story and were later displayed in the classroom.

During a following session the children painted key aspects of the setting, enabling further visualisation. These were used as illustrations for a class book.

section three

Books that offer a range of characters/animals, and different settings, are ideal for visualising, for example *Angry Arthur* by Hiawyn Oram and Satoshi Kitamura or *Handa's Surprise* by Eileen Browne.

Vignette Year 1 *Visualising*

With his Year 1 class, this teacher wanted to use drama as a basis for encouraging the children to visualise what they read. He decided to use this anonymous poem. *

That... is... the... one...
This is the one,
That is the one,
This is the one, that is the one
This is the one, that is the one...
This... is... the... one
Over the river, past the mill
Through the tunnel under the hill;
Round the corner, past the wall,
Through the wood where trees grow tall
Then in sight of the town by the river,
Brake by the crossing where white leaves quiver.
Slow as the streets of the town slide past
And the windows stare
At the jerking of the coaches
Coming into the station approaches.
Stop at the front
Stop at the front
Stop... at the front
Stop... at the...
Stop

Ahhh!

Without telling the children that the poem was about a train, he read it to them and asked what it was about. Several of them noticed the rhythmic reading and the mention of a station and suggested it might be about a train. Then the teacher asked the children to recall some of the places the poem mentioned. As they gave him their ideas he wrote the place on a piece of A4 paper - 'over the river', 'into the station' (deliberately including the preposition) and placed it on the floor in the sequence that the poem took. He was careful to leave space for any details the children had left out and when he re-read the poem he asked them to notice any places they had missed. When they had identified all the key places, he asked the children in groups to go to each spot and imagine they were people who were going about their everyday business there. What might they be doing? He gave them some examples: children paddling or fishing in the river; the miller grinding corn and farmers who had brought their corn to be ground; people picnicking on the hill; children sitting on the wall waving to the train… and asked them to think up more things they could be doing. One group of children were the train, with driver and passengers. After a little while for discussion, he asked the groups to freeze so that they made tableaux of each scene. He quickly took digital photographs of them which he uploaded on the IWB and used as prompts for the children to sequence the events of the poem.

* *I haven't been able to find the author of this poem and give proper credit. If anyone knows, please let me know.*

section three comprehension

Once the children were clear about the sequence, he asked them to close their eyes and visualise the train's journey, checking that all had some kind of picture in their mind's eye. He explained to them that it is rare, but can happen, that an individual does not visualise what they read or hear. This isn't a problem, just a part of that person's thinking processes. As long as they are working with a person who does visualise, that's fine. He asked them also to consider:

What might you see when you are going over the river?
What might you hear when you are going through the wood?
What do the streets of the town look like?

Finally, he asked each child to select a part of the train's journey they had a particularly clear image of and to draw it. The children's drawings were displayed with their frozen tableaux photographs as a basis for further work about journeys with a teaching focus on prepositions.

'Journey' poems always offer a range of settings, and characters, for visualising and drama work. Find them on the Children's Poetry Archive website at: http://childrenspoetryarchive.org/

Vignette Year 2 *Visualising*

As part of a unit of work where children were exploring settings in texts, this Year 2 teacher used the book *The Worst Witch* by Jill Murphy to focus on how the setting is described on the opening page. She read the passage which describes the setting of Miss Cackle's Academy for Witches on page 1.

The teacher then read it again and as she did so, the children were asked to visualise it. The teacher repeated the reading and this time the children were asked to draw what they saw. She then selected several which she displayed on the visualiser for the class to see. Drawings were compared and key vocabulary, such as 'gloomy', 'turrets' and 'winding' discussed.

The children then completed 'Tell me/Show me' grids outlining what they could see and hear in the setting.

Tell me	Show me	
	I can see	*I can hear*
Miss Cackle's Academy for Witches		

Their notes were then used as a basis for the children writing their own descriptions of Miss Cackle's Academy.

Chapter stories are ideal for visualising. Almost every story starts by describing a setting.

Questioning

Asking questions before, during and after reading is fundamental to reaching a deeper understanding about what is being read. Experienced readers do this automatically and unconsciously. Children are often asked to respond to questions generated by the teacher, but it is important that children themselves pose questions in order to understand or clarify the content of what they are reading. These questions can be literal, where pupils locate specific information, inferential where they read between the lines, or evaluative where they assess content through their own opinions or judgements.

Aidan Chambers (2011) suggests that questions fall into the three categories, literal, opinion-related and inferential.

section three

Literal questions

Many literal questions will start with 'what', 'how', 'when' and 'where' and will be direct questions, generally looking for facts, for example:

What did the boy do...?
What is in...?
What do you notice about...?
What happened when...?
What does the picture show...?
How did the girl...?
How did the boy explain...?
When did...?
Where can you find...?

Opinion-related questions

These are often questions asking for reasons, either based on the text or on personal experience. They require selecting specific parts of the text, for example:

Which parts of the book/poem did you like best/find most moving/scary...?
Which sections gave you the most interesting information?
Do you know anyone like the boy in the story?
Have you ever felt like the girl felt when...?
How did the character change as the story went on?
Could... really have happened?
If you had been the mother, what would you have done?

Inferential questions

These are generally more 'open' or conditional, for example:

What do you think might happen...?
What do you think the boy should do?
What could the girl say to help her friend?
How could you tell from the girl's expression that...?
How might the old woman...?
How do you know...?
When did the illustrator first show us...?

Recommended Teaching Approaches
Vignette Year R *Questioning*

As part of a unit of work, this Reception teacher used *The Rainbow Fish* by Marcus Pfister to focus on the main character in order to discuss key characteristics. With the children gathered on the carpet, he showed them the front cover of the book and asked them to discuss what they noticed about the Rainbow Fish. He generated from them that *Rainbow Fish had shiny scales*. The teacher then explained that the other fish in the story wanted to share the shiny scales but the rainbow fish wouldn't. He asked the children why they thought the fish wouldn't share and they responded with: *because they were his, because he is mean, because he wanted them all to himself*.

The teacher then read the story to the children. He displayed a large puppet of the rainbow fish which he sat on his knee. He explained to the children that they were going to find out more about the rainbow fish so they had to think of some questions to ask him. The teacher demonstrated this by asking 'is it nice having lots of friends?'

section three comprehension

> With their talk partners, the children devised questions for the Rainbow Fish such as *Do you like your scales? What do you eat? Do you like living in the water?*
>
> The teaching assistant then went into role as the Rainbow Fish and the children asked their questions.
>
> The teacher scribed some responses on the flipchart ready for use in shared writing in the next session.

Any picturebook with a strong central character and a storyline that shows the character's relationship with others is good for developing questioning of this sort.

> ### Vignette Year 1 *Questioning*
>
> A Year 1 teacher wanted to encourage her class to ask questions about the books they were reading. She used Martin Waddell's *The Pig in the Pond* for one extended session of about an hour. She read them the story and then as she re-read it, she asked the children in pairs to think of questions they would like to ask Farmer Neligan. She then explained that Farmer Neligan was going to write a letter to his friend Farmer Hoggart telling him about what had happened when he got home from market, so that the children would need to find out how he felt about the day's events to help him write his letter. The exciting thing was that they were just about to meet Farmer Neligan (the teaching assistant in farmer costume) so they could question him.
>
> Farmer Neligan was hot-seated and the children asked:
>
> *What had you been doing that day?*
> *Had you had a good day or were you in a grumpy mood?*
> *Were you surprised when you got back to the farm?*
> *What did you feel when you saw the pig in the pond?*
> *Why did you decide to jump in?*
> *Had you ever jumped in the pond before?*
> *Was it dangerous to jump in the pond?*
>
> The teacher scribed the answers so that the children had a frame for writing Farmer Neligan's letter to Farmer Hoggart telling him about the day's adventures.

Questioning can be developed just as well by using an extract from a film where the focus is on the central character who has a dilemma/problem to solve. Many films that the children will have seen at home have such episodes and strong central characters that can be hot seated to find out about their feelings and motives.

> ### Vignette Year 2 *Questioning*
>
> Over the course of a week, a Year 2 class teacher spent four thirty minute sessions reading Anthony Browne's *The Tunnel*. She used the visualiser so that the children could pore over the rich pictorial text carefully. First, they looked at the cover of the book and with the teacher modelling the kind of questions that might be asked, came up with some prompted by the cover:
>
> *Who is the girl?*
> *How is she feeling?*
> *Where might the tunnel lead?*
>
> Together, the class looked at the first few double page spreads to where the boy goes into the tunnel. The teacher asked them to think about whether any of their initial questions had been

answered. They decided they knew what the girl was like - that she liked reading and didn't like rough games - and that she had a brother and a mum. They thought that she was feeling scared, but hadn't quite reached the point in the story depicted on the cover and they didn't yet know where the tunnel led. The session ended on that cliff-hanger - as she entered the tunnel. On the next day, before they started to look at the book again, the teacher asked them in pairs to come up with one extra question that they wanted to ask. They wrote their questions on small slips of paper and put them in a box labelled 'Not to be opened until we have read the book'.

The class then looked at the rest of the story on the visualiser. After they had read the whole story, the teacher asked the children in their pairs to choose one of the questions from the box and to discuss whether it had been answered or not. Some of the questions that had been answered were:

Was she frightened to go through the tunnel?

Will there be a witch there?

Will she find her brother?

But some questions remained unanswered:

Why did her brother go into the tunnel?

Why did he tease her so much?

What are her favourite books?

Why is there a witch's hat on the wardrobe?

In the following week the children developed a story 'Further adventures down the tunnel' and tried to deal with all the questions that had remained unanswered.

Many complex picturebooks - where the pictures need a lot of poring over - lend themselves well to developing questioning. Pairs of children could each take a double page spread and develop their own questions about what is going on in the picture.

Connecting

In order to infer meaning from texts, children need to make connections between their own lives, other texts and their knowledge and understanding of the world. Along with the evaluative - viewpoints and personal beliefs - these connections are key to gaining deeper understanding of what is being read. It allows for the reader to connect with the writer and take meaning from what is not written on the page.

There are three types of connections:

Text-to-self connections: These enable children to draw directly on their own personal experiences and lives: *This is a story about a dog. Do you have a dog at home?*

Text-to-text connections: These enable children to draw upon their knowledge about other stories: *This is a story about a giant. What do we know about giants from other stories we have read?*

Text-to-world connections: These require children to have a knowledge and understanding of the world beyond their own experiences: *In this story Baby Bear goes to the moon. What do you know about the moon? What might he see there?*

When making connections it is important to ask questions such as:

What is the same?

What is different?

What does it remind you of?

section three comprehension

Recommended Teaching Approaches
Vignette Year R *Connecting text-to-self*

With the children gathered on the carpet, this Year R teacher gave an overview of the story *Lima's Red Hot Chilli* by David Mills. As part of the overview, he showed the children a real red chilli explaining to them that it was very hot. He broke the chilli in half and showed the children the tiny seeds inside explaining that the seeds were even hotter, so you have to remember to scrape them away before you eat the chilli.

He showed the children the front cover of the text with the illustration of Lima having eaten the chilli. He asked the children whether they thought Lima had scraped away the tiny seeds. Following a brief discussion, he read the text to the children then explored with them why Lima should have listened to her mum.

In order to help the children create text-to-self connections he then asked the children, in pairs, to discuss times when they themselves had been naughty. He took feedback encouraging the children to say what the consequences of their actions were.

To help support text-to-self connections it is best to choose a story with a familiar setting and a main event that could happen to any child.

Vignette Year 1 *Connecting text-to-self*

As part of a unit of work culminating in writing a class book, this Year 1 teacher was using the book *Mr Gumpy's Outing* by John Burningham as a basis for the class to write their own version of the story with an alternative setting. During the first session she had read the story to the children and retold it using visuals. In this session, she explained to the children that they were going to write their own version of *Mr Gumpy's Outing* but this time Mr Gumpy's boat was going on a river in the jungle.

Referring them back to previous work on *Elmer* by David McKee, she asked the children, with their talk partners, to think about animals that live in the jungle that might go on an outing with Mr Gumpy. They suggested several possibilities and she selected two or three animals and developed ideas about how they move, again asking the children to make connections with other texts read. She scribed examples on the flipchart:

Monkeys	*jump/swing*
Elephants	*tramp*
Lions	*crouch/leap*

The teacher then chose groups of five children in turn to come to the middle of the circle to role play the animals and their movements, taking digital pictures of each group.

During the following session, she displayed the photographs and the children developed ideas about the jungle setting, leading to making a class book.

Text-to-text connections are best developed if you use a picturebook or a poem that links to other stories the children have read. For role play activities, a range of characters also helps.

Vignette Year 2 *Connecting text-to-text*

As part of a unit of work looking at giants in texts, this Year 2 teacher asked the children to work in pairs to discuss what they knew about giants in stories they have read or films they have seen. She explained to the children that they should remember stories such as *Jack and the Beanstalk* by Richard Walker, *Jim and the Beanstalk* by Raymond Briggs, *The Selfish Giant* by Michael Foreman/Oscar Wilde, *The Smartest Giant in Town* by Julia Donaldson and *The BFG* by Roald Dahl. Following their discussion the children gave feedback and the teacher noted the characteristics generated by the children on the flipchart under the heading 'What we know about giants'.

| What we know about giants | What is the same? | What is different? |

The teacher then read *Giant Hiccups* by Jacqui Farley to the children and they then discussed, in pairs, the central character of the giant. How was this giant the same as other giants and how was she different? As the children made suggestions she filled in the second and third columns on the flipchart.

These notes were used for the children to refer to when they wrote their own character sketches of 'A giant who is different'.

There is a lot of scope for making text-to-text connections from children's home reading and film experience of typical character type(s) in traditional stories, for example, giants, witches, princesses, heroes.

Inferring

Inferring is about drawing out the implicit meaning in the text, supplying information not provided explicitly by the author, but hinted at - reading between the lines and creating personal links to what the author has written. In order to infer, children need a wide range of vocabulary, real and imagined experiences and knowledge of people and the world around them. Often children learn about character, settings and events from watching films and television and develop inference skills that can be built on in reading print.

Recommended Teaching Approaches
Vignette Year R *Inferring*

As part of a thematic approach to cross curricular work, this Reception teacher used the film clip *Baboon on the Moon* (BFI Education, 2004) as the stimulus for a range of learning opportunities, including developing reading comprehension for literacy. In a previous session, she had shown the film, without interruption, to the children.

At the beginning of this session, she explained that they were going to watch the film again but this time she wanted them to be thinking about how Baboon was feeling. Following this, the children, with their talk partners, discussed their ideas. They replied: *he was sad, he was lonely, he missed his mum*, etc.

She showed the film again, this time in small sections. She wanted the children to give reasons for how they thought Baboon was feeling. At the end of each section the teacher paused the film and discussed with the children what they thought. They suggested:

He was lonely because no-one else was there. He was sad because he was crying. He wanted a friend because he kept looking at his home.

Finally, she focused on the music at the end and how it made them feel. They responded with:

It makes me feel sad. It's slow and sad.

In further sessions, the teacher generated questions, such as:

How did Baboon get to the moon? How could he get home? What could he do to feel happier?

This developed children's understanding further and also supported cross curricular work related to the film.

section three comprehension

Almost every commercially made animated film has an episode where the character has to make a decision - often a moral one. Select a short sequence where the camera shows some close-up shots of the main character as well as some scene-setting longer shots. This can be an introduction to later viewing of the whole film.

Vignette Year 1 *Inferring*

Combining PSHE and reading sessions, this Year 1 teacher read *John Brown, Rose and the Midnight Cat* by Jenny Wagner with her class. She had uploaded some images from the book on to the IWB as a focus for discussion. When she got to the section where Rose put out the milk for the Midnight Cat and John Brown tipped it out, she stopped reading and asked the children, in pairs, to discuss why he was doing that. They fed back ideas about him feeling jealous and she listed these on the flipchart. One of the children suggested that he had felt safe at first because Rose had said 'We're all right', suggesting that she didn't need any more company than John Brown, but now she wanted the cat as well. Before reading on, the teacher showed the children images of some of the pages where John Brown refuses to look at the cat and asked them if they could find any evidence from the illustrations that John Brown felt jealous. They told her that refusing to look at the cat and drawing a line round the house told them that he didn't like the cat.

While they were discussing John Brown's feelings, the teacher asked the children if they had ever felt jealous and several volunteered their own experiences of feeling put out of place by a younger sibling, or of not being invited to someone's party. She explained that their own experiences helped them to understand John Brown's feelings.

As they listened to the rest of the story, the children jotted down extra evidence of John Brown's jealousy and unhappiness. Some of this was drawn from the words of the book, some from the illustrations and some from the children's feelings of empathy with him. When the story was finished, the teacher asked the children to think about how Rose had dealt with John Brown's feelings and to talk to each other in pairs about whether she had done the right thing. She reminded the children that they should be able to give a reason for what they were saying; it might be from the words of the book, from the pictures or from their own experience. As they fed back their thoughts, if they forgot to give their reasons she asked: 'What makes you think that?' so that they began to internalise the idea that opinions based on inference need to have some kind of backing from the text or from experience of the world.

Developing inference can often be linked to other areas of the curriculum. A text with a focus on a character's emotions links well with PSHE but you could also choose texts to fit with science, maths, history or geography, for example.

Vignette Year 2 *Inferring*

As part of a unit of work based on the text *Amazing Grace* by Mary Hoffman, this Year 2 teacher wanted the children to use evidence from the text to consider the central character, Grace. With the children sitting on the carpet, the teacher produced a suitcase containing various articles (doll, story books, ribbons, hair clips, notebook and pen, dressing up clothes and a DVD of Peter Pan). Slowly he opened the suitcase revealing one by one the artefacts inside. As he pulled each one out he asked the children to be thinking about who might own the suitcase. He displayed the artefacts on a table at the front of the class.

The teacher had written three key questions in a chart on the board:

section three

Questions	Responses
1. Who might this suitcase belong to?	
2. What makes you think that?	
3. What do the objects tell you about this character?	

In pairs, the children then discussed who they thought would own such possessions and what sort of person they might be. Following their paired discussion, the children gave feedback to the teacher who wrote their responses in the second column. He then explained that he was going to read them a story about the character who actually does own the suitcase. He explained that although the artefacts gave them clues as to what the character was like, there will be other clues in the text which they should listen out for. The children then added to the list of characteristics and the teacher kept the list as a basis for future work.

In a later session the teacher asked the children what treasured objects they might pack in their own suitcases or boxes. He read them Kit Wright's poem 'The Magic Box' and they wrote their own poems based on their treasured possessions.

Making up a small suitcase, a box or bag with some belongings of the central character is an ideal way of starting a unit of work based on a particular text. Work on inferring like this could lead to the children making or describing their own 'suitcases' or boxes of things they treasure, forming the basis for personal writing.

Key question

What texts have you and your colleagues found useful for developing the range of comprehension strategies:

    Summarising

    Predicting

    Visualising

    Questioning

    Connecting

    Inferring?

It might be worth collating these as a useful resource, adding to the list as you find new texts.

section four assessing reading

Types of assessment

There are two main types of assessment of children's progress in reading: summative and formative, or continuous assessment.

Summative assessments are records of what children have learned and they are taken at the end of a period of instruction. Children are judged against national standards or benchmarks periodically throughout the year. This could be termly, half termly or indeed more frequently. Although some summative assessments can be used formatively, they are, by and large, used to monitor the progress of cohorts of children and to predict end of key stage attainment. Summative assessment can be defined as assessment *of* learning.

Formative/ continuous assessments - assessments *for* learning - on the other hand are ongoing and are designed to monitor a pupil's learning at the point at which it happens. These assessments give the teacher an opportunity to recognise gaps in understanding and allow them to address those gaps through revisiting key concepts where necessary. They also offer opportunities to identify pupils' strengths and weaknesses and provide feedback that can move learning forward. Formative assessment can also be diagnostic, helping to identify groups of children who may require extra support through further assessment and interventions.

> *Assessment for learning is the process of seeking and interpreting evidence for use by learners and their teachers to decide where the learners are in their learning, where they need to go and how best to get there.*
> (Assessment Reform Group, 2012:2)

> *When we measure outcomes of teaching with tests, the instruction of the learners is already over. In legal terms, we would say that the test score comes 'after the fact.' It is almost too late to change the fate of pupils based on what these scores reveal. We no longer have the opportunity to do that. The opportunity has gone.* (Clay, 2006:5)

Only formative, ongoing teacher assessment will give the detailed insight needed to show where children are in terms of their reading development. Summative assessments in the form of tests of different kinds do not give the kind of information needed to identify key issues and plan for teaching that will move children's reading forward.

Assessment at different stages of reading progress

It is possible to identify five key developmental stages in children's reading progression: Emergent, Early, Transitional, Self-extending and Advanced (Fountas and Pinnell, 1996; Caravette, 2011). As children move through these stages, the emphasis on what the teacher assesses changes.

Emergent, Early and Transitional readers

There are two focuses of assessment for children at these levels: decoding and comprehension.

In terms of decoding, it is important to find out:

- what sources of information children are using and whether they are over-reliant on just one source
- what reading strategies children are using to process this information: whether they are using a range of strategies, such as re-reading, reading on, cross checking (early on) or whether they are over-using just one, such as sounding words out
- children's reading behaviours: is one to one correspondence secure? Is the child reading fluently?

In terms of comprehension, it is important that the teacher finds out if children can:

- retell simple stories or events and summarise them
- make predictions before, during and after reading
- make connections, particularly text-to-self connections, linking what they read or hear read to their own experiences
- generate and respond to questions some of which may require them to make predictions and inferences based on the text. (see pages 63 and 71 Section 3)

The level at which the children are reading will influence what the teacher has to assess. For example, a child beginning to read would not be expected to have a wide range of strategies nor would they necessarily be able to generate sophisticated questions. However, a child reading further along the continuum, for example, at the Transitional stage, would be expected to have these in place.

Self-extending readers

Children reading at the self-extending level and beyond, would primarily be assessed on comprehension alone. It is important for the teacher to establish that children can use a range of comprehension strategies at a sophisticated level. Other aspects of reading such as whether children can comment on writers' use of language, whether they can identify and comment on literary features, derive information from non-fiction texts, will also need assessing.

What needs to be assessed?

Figure 4.1 (over the page) summarises what needs to be assessed in terms of comprehension at each stage of the early reading continuum.

Collecting evidence

There is a variety of evidence that can be checked against national curriculum programmes of study to provide information to the teacher about the child as a reader. Some evidence can be used both formatively and summatively. The two most significant are:

- Guided Reading records which are mainly used formatively but can provide evidence for overall end of year judgements.
- Running records which can be used both formatively and summatively.

A range of other evidence can be gathered by teachers. This could include letter/sound tests, word tests, dictated sentence tests (hearing and recording sounds in words), writing samples, for example, character descriptions, and reading age tests.

Teachers will also draw on observations they make on their pupils' reading, including children's habits and preferences. These would be done during read aloud sessions, Shared Reading lessons and independent reading times, through noticing choices children make and examining home school reading journals and responses. These observations go towards the teacher's overall understanding of the child as a reader and will complement and also may help to explain the child's progress as measured by tests. These observations can usefully inform curricular decisions about reading provision.

Guided Reading records

Guided Reading records are a powerful source of formative, teacher assessment which are completed following direct instruction. They represent a record of the teacher's observations from focused reading sessions. Although these records contain essential information such as the names of the children, targets, texts and possibly prompts (see page 27 Section 1) they also contain notes about children's progress towards the targets set.

Notes should be made both during the direct teaching part of the lesson and when children are reading independently. At this point the teacher should 'key' in to individual children to assess their reading. Annotations on the Guided Reading record sheet should be made 'on the run' and not at some later time after the session is finished.

section four assessing reading

Emergent Pre band 1, Bands 1 and 2	Early Bands 3,4,5, 6	Transitional Bands 7,8,9	Self-extending Band 10
Whether children can: read and understand simple sentences demonstrate understanding when talking with others about what they have read recognise one or two words in different contexts understand and use simple terminology such as book, right way up, front, back, upside down understand that print goes from left to right including return sweep understand that the left page comes before the right know that print (not the picture) tells the story know that there are letters, and clusters of letters called words understand that there are first letters and last letters in words match one to one.	Whether children: know that print conveys meaning - what they read makes sense know how language is written down: the grammatical structure, including punctuation - what they read sounds right grammatically know about visual information: - phonics - graphic information including word endings and words of more than one syllable know and apply of a range of reading strategies: - self-monitoring - self-correcting - orchestrating all sources of information - cross checking meaning and visual information.	Whether children: use context of what they read to decode control more complex and varied grammatical structures use a wider range of visual information including prefixes, suffixes and syllabification know and apply of a range of reading strategies: - self-monitoring - self-correcting - orchestrating all sources of information - re-reading - reading on.	Whether children: use context of what they read to decode control more complex and varied grammatical structures use a wider range of visual information including prefixes, suffixes and syllabification know and apply of a range of reading strategies: - self-monitoring - self-correcting - orchestrating all sources of information - re-reading - reading on.
Whether children can: express themselves effectively, showing awareness of listeners' needs use vocabulary and forms of speech that are increasingly influenced by their experience of books use simple grammatical structures orally.	Whether children can: read fluently read with expression.	Whether children can: read fluently read with expression begin to read silently.	Whether children can: read fluently read with expression read silently.
Whether children can: understand literally what has been read and sequence key events reach a deeper understanding of what has been read by using a range of reading comprehension strategies: - summarising (retelling) - predicting (before reading) - visualising (simple settings) - questioning (responding) - connecting (text-to-self).	Whether children can: understand literally what has been read and sequence key events reach a deeper understanding of what has been read by using a range of reading comprehension strategies: - summarising (key events) - predicting (before and during reading) - visualising (settings) - questioning (responding and generating) - connecting (text-to-self, text-to-text) understand and describe information.	Whether children can: reach a deeper understanding of what has been read by using a range of reading comprehension strategies: - summarising (key events) - predicting (before, during and after reading) - visualising (settings, characters) - questioning (responding and generating) - connecting (text-to-self, text-to-text, text-to-world) - inferring (reading between the lines) understand, describe, select or retrieve information.	Whether children can: reach a deeper understanding of what has been read by using a range of reading comprehension strategies: - summarising (key events) - predicting (before, during and after reading) - visualising (settings, characters) - questioning (responding and generating) - connecting (text-to-self, text-to-text, text-to-world) - inferring (reading between the lines) understand, describe, select or retrieve information, events or ideas from texts and begin to use quotations and references from the text explain and comment on writers' use of language, including some grammatical and some literary features identify and comment on writers' purposes and viewpoints and the overall effect of the text on the reader relate texts to their social, cultural and historical contexts.

Left: Figure 4.1 Assessment at each stage of the Early Reading continuum.
(See Appendix for photocopiable proforma Planning and Target Setting for Guided Reading.)

In order to keep these records, teachers need to develop almost a 'shorthand' so that they can keep pace with the children. These can be simple annotations which merely show that the teacher has seen evidence that the child has met or partially met the target. Such as:

T1 ✓ (Target 1 evidence seen)

To add more detail, observations can be noted using the format for running record assessments (see page 79). For example:

for miscues or self-corrections:

there	bee	sc
these	beetle	

for sources of information used:

To make comments on reading behaviours, abbreviations can be used, such as:

finger pointing 'f/p'

fluency 'fl' (good)   **fluency** 'fl' (not good).

It is also important to make notes on observations about reading comprehension. In the early stages, there is likely to be just one reading comprehension target, such as making text-to-self connections. It is useful to know if the teacher has seen evidence of children being able to do this. Again it could be a simple annotation such as:

T3 ✓ (Target 3 evidence seen).

However, where possible, it is useful to write direct quotes from the children as further evidence of comprehension skills. Such as:

I've been to a farm too and I saw different animals.

Running records

The most successful way of assessing the key elements of the reading process - sources of information, reading strategies and behaviours - is by taking running record assessments and applying three levels of analysis to assess:

- what information pupils are using when they read
- whether they are over-reliant on just one source
- the independent reading strategies children are deploying, for example, whether pupils make meaning errors which they then check against their phonological knowledge or graphic information
- reading behaviours such as consistency of one-to-one correspondence, fluency and phrasing.

Running records are contextual assessments which measure children's independent application skills. In the same way as teachers look at samples to assess writing, they will look at running records to assess reading. Running records provide the teacher with the most in-depth knowledge of children's processing competence. For example, when assessing the use of visual information, running records can be more informative than run-of-the-mill word lists or phoneme checks, because they show teachers whether the children can apply their knowledge in the context of reading.

Running records look for children's accurate reading and errors, for example:

- substitutions made for words in the text
- repetitions of words
- self-corrections
- insertions of words not in the original text

section four assessing reading

- words that the child needed to be told
- if the child looks (appeals) to the teacher for help.

After noting these, the teacher then analyses the accurate and miscued words to identify the sources of information and reading strategies the child is using.

> *Tests of alphabet knowledge, phonics, phonemic awareness, and sight words form part of reading assessment but they don't provide the whole picture of how a student approaches the reading process. Gathering information from a running record, which gives a reliable and valid assessment of text reading, and adding this information to other assessments enables a teacher to gain a richer and more comprehensive assessment of a student's reading ability.* (Government of South Australia, 2014: 1)

Taking a running record

As a general rule, running record assessments should be carried out once or twice a year. The exception to this would be if a child or group of children are not making progress. It would then be necessary to benchmark them more frequently in order to continually monitor and unpick what is 'getting in the way' for them.

Where possible, running record assessments should be taken by the teacher in a quiet area away from the classroom. The teacher will have prepared a running record sheet with the text the child is to read, set out sentence by sentence, on the left hand side and with columns for annotations on the right (Figure 4.2). The child should sit next to the teacher who will give a brief overview of the text about to be read; this should be one that the child has not met before. The overview should not be detailed but could include the title of the book, attention to any tricky or technical words unfamiliar to the child or any proper nouns, especially names of characters which might appear several times in the text.

> *Taking running records of children's reading behaviour requires time and practice, but the results are well worth the effort. Once learned, the running record is a quick, practical and highly informative tool. It becomes an integral part of teaching, not only for documenting children's reading behaviours for later analysis and reflection but sharpening the teacher's observational power and understanding of the reading process.* (Fountas and Pinnell, 1996: 89)

section four

Running Record Assessment				
Text: *Hedgehog is Hungry* by Beverley Randell				
Name:		**Date:**		
Running Words **Errors** **Self correction rate**	Accuracy		Errors	Self-correction
Page	E	SC	E msv	SC msv
3 Winter is here.				
5 Hedgehog is asleep.				
7 Spring is here. Hedgehog wakes up.				
9 Here comes Hedgehog.				
11 Hedgehog is hungry. Here is a snail.				

13 Hedgehog is hungry.
     Here is a worm.
     Here is a caterpillar.				

15 Here is a beetle. Here is a slug.				
16 Hedgehog is hungry in the spring.				

Figure 4.2 Running record sheet.

Following the introduction, the child would then read to the teacher who would annotate the running record sheet according to the conventions shown in Figure 4.3.

section four assessing reading

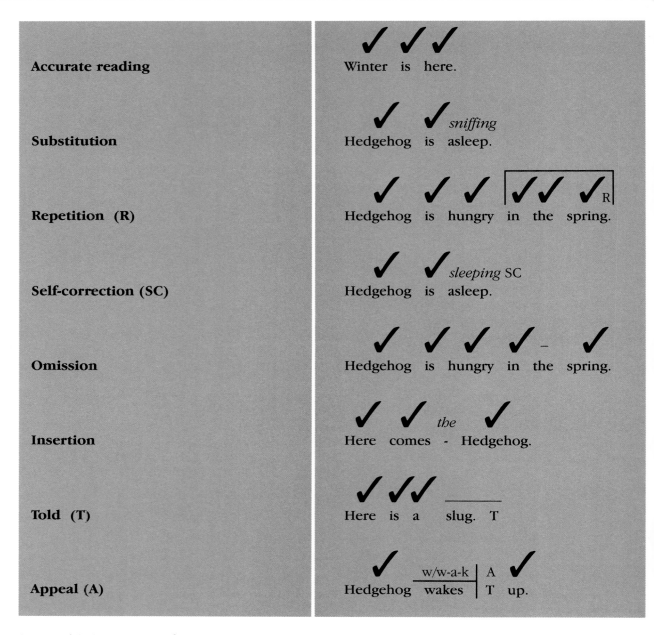

Figure 4.3 Conventions for annotating running records

The teacher should also note any key reading behaviours such as finger pointing or fluency issues on the record sheet.

Taking the running record is an opportunity for the teacher to observe the child, NOT to engage in teaching. It enables analysis of what the child is doing as a reader and what they are not doing.

Once the running record has been taken the teacher will then carry out the three levels of analysis.

Three levels of analysis of a running record

First level analysis – instructional reading level

The first level of analysis calculates the instructional reading level (Book Band) of the child. To indicate an instructional level, the running record will show an accuracy rate of between 90% and 94%. A running record accuracy rate of between 95% and 100% means that the text is too easy and an accuracy rate of below 90% means that the text is too hard for the reader. A 'too easy' running record assessment will mean that there is not enough information for the teacher to analyse. 'Too hard' suggests that the children will often have lost the support of the meaning of the text, and so the assessment is skewed.

section four

It is therefore important to ensure that a running record shows an instructional level as this will allow the teacher to determine the selection of texts for Guided Reading sessions. However, the running record alone will not always support the choice of targets, as children may have differing needs, see, for example, Bradley and Suzy on page 82.

The first stage of analysis involves quantifying the running record and calculating the child's self-correction rate, to determine whether the text being used is at an instructional level or not (for details see page 83). First of all the uncorrected errors need to be counted and divided into the total number of words in the passage; this gives the error frequency. This is then subtracted from the number of errors to give the percentage of accuracy, and finally the self-correction rate is calculated by adding self-corrections and errors together and dividing by the self-corrections.

Second level analysis - sources of information

The second level of analysis will inform the teacher what sources of information are being used by the child at the point of error and what they are using when they self-correct. For example whether the child is predominately using meaning to correct errors or whether they are able to use all three sources – meaning, structure and visual. The teacher will do this by initially writing 'm','s' and 'v' next to each error and then analyse the miscue. They will make the analysis by circling the source of information used by the child. When analysing visual information, the teacher can add further detail by looking at what part of the word the child attended to, using the annotations: i (initial); m (middle); f (final). The analysis must be done up to the point in the text where the error was made. The whole sentence should not be taken in to account.

The teacher will then do the same for the self-corrections, analysing the error in the first instance and then the self-correction. What source/sources of information did the child use to correct the miscue?

Third level of analysis - reading strategies

The third level of analysis, which is perhaps the most productive, allows teachers to look at the reading strategies the child is using (see Section Three page 61). This is often an indicator of how independent, or not, the child is as a reader.

Examples of reading strategies are:

- Self-monitoring
- Self-correcting
- Re-reading
- Reading on
- Cross checking (checking one sources with another - usually meaning with visual information, initial letter sounds)
- Searching for information
- Orchestrating all sources of information (using meaning, structure and visual information altogether to make meaning).

This level of analysis enables the teacher to look at how children are actually processing the information the print is giving them. It shows whether the child has a range of strategies or whether they are over reliant on one, like sounding words out. The more strategies a child uses, the more self-extending they tend to be.

The following extended Case Study shows how a teacher used all three levels of analysis of running records to plan for teaching.

section four assessing reading

Case study Assessing Bradley's and Suzy's reading - moving into instruction

As part of regular assessments, Jan, a Year 1 teacher, carried out running records with Guided Reading Blue Group (see Section One page 27). Two records are described in detail here. Bradley, a 6 year old boy, was reading at Book Band 2 (Figure 4.4).

Running Record Assessment

Text: *Hedgehog is Hungry* by Beverley Randell

Name: Bradley **Date: October 16th**

Running Words 47 Errors 4 Self correction rate 1.5	Accuracy 92%	Errors	Self-correction

Page		E	SC	E msv	SC msv
3	✓ ✓ ✓ Winter is here.				
5	✓ ✓ ✓ Hedgehog is asleep.				
7	✓ ✓ ✓ Spring is here.				
	✓ w/w-a-k A Hedgehog wakes T up.	1		m s (v)	
	He sc ✓ ✓				
9	Here comes Hedgehog.		1	(m)(s)(v_i)	m s (v)
11	✓ ✓ hunting Hedgehog is hungry.	1		(m)(s)(v) i/m	
	✓ ✓ ✓ ✓ Here is a snail.				
13	✓ ✓ ✓ Hedgehog is hungry.				
	✓ ✓ ✓ w/w-o A Here is a worm. T	1		m s (v)	
	✓ ✓ ✓ ✓ Here is a caterpillar.				
15	✓ ✓ ✓ b/bee ✓ Here is a beetle.				
	✓ ✓ ✓ s/s-l/ A Here is a slug. T	1		m s (v)	
16	✓ ✓ ✓ ✓ ✓ Hedgehog is hungry in the spring.				
		4	1	2 2 4	0 0 1

82

Left: Figure 4.4 Bradley's running record assessment

(**i** = initial letter[s]; **m** = middle letters; **f** = final letters)

Jan carried out the first level of analysis (see below) by calculating whether Bradley was reading at an instructional level or whether the text was too easy or too hard. She did this by taking the number of errors made, in this case four, and dividing them by the number of words read, in this case 47. This gave an accuracy level of 1:12 - for every 12 words read, Bradley made 1 error, which Jan calculated as giving him an instructional level of 92%. She noted that Bradley had self-corrected once and so she worked out the self-correction rate by taking the number of self-corrections: 1 and adding it to the number of errors: 4 to give a total number of errors of 5. She divided the total number of errors by the number of self-corrections: 5 ÷ 1 = 5 thus giving Bradley a self-correction rate of 1:5.

Step	What to do	Calculation
1	Count the number of words.	47
2	Count the number of uncorrected errors.	4
3	Divide the number of words by the number of uncorrected errors made.	47 ÷ 4 = 12
4	Find the error rate.	1.12
5	Make it into a percentage (using a calculator if necessary).	92%
6	Add the number of self- corrections.	1
7	Find the self-correction rate by adding the errors and the self-corrected errors together.	4 + 1 = 5
8	Find the self-correction rate by dividing the total number of errors [uncorrected and corrected] by the number of self-corrections.	5 ÷ 1 = 5 Self-correction rate of 1:5

She then went on to carry out the second level of analysis. She needed to know what sources of information Bradley was able to use independently. She noted that Bradley used meaning and structure twice and visual information four times at the point of error. He was, therefore, over-reliant on visual information particularly sounding words out using a phoneme by phoneme approach.

w/w-a-k | A

Awakes |

w-o-r | A
---
worm |

s/s-l/
---
slug

He did attend to meaning, substituting a word that would make sense in the context of the piece:

hunting
---
hungry

Structure was sound when it was used but he did not attend to meaning or structure when making phoneme by phoneme approaches to words.

section four assessing reading

The third level of analysis revealed that Bradley had a tendency to appeal to the adult when sounding out didn't work. He was self-monitoring and did self-correct by using visual information possibly graphic (high frequency words) information:

$$\frac{he}{here}$$

Jan noticed that Bradley's reading was not fluent especially as he used sounding out as his main strategy. He still had a tendency to point to each word.

As a result of her analysis of the running record, she decided that she needed to help Bradley work on using meaning consistently, checking this against the visual information he was keen on using. He needed to develop his fluency beginning with two and three word phrases, such as: 'here is a' or: '*said mum*' '*said the boy*'.

Jan then analysed Suzy's assessment (Figure 4.5). She was in the same Guided Reading group as Bradley so the same text was appropriate.

The first level of analysis for both children was identical (see Figure 4.6). But the second and third levels, by contrast, showed that Suzy was using predominantly meaning and structure. She did not always attend to visual information including initial letter sounds, although like Bradley, she was self-monitoring and correcting using visual information. She did not always cross check meaning with the initial letters and her reading lacked fluency.

Based on all this information and other assessments carried out, (Figure 4.7) Jan chose targets for the group to support:

- the consistent use of cross checking ensuring that both meaning and visual information were attended to
- increased knowledge of high frequency words and to help develop fluency.

Jan completed a Guided Reading proforma to help her plan for instruction (Figure 4.8).

After six weeks the proforma had a great deal of information about Blue Group's progress (Figure 4.9) and she decided to carry out a further running record assessment on Bradley as she wanted to ensure that he was able to read instructionally at the next band. This would act as a benchmark for the whole group (Figure 4.10). She compared the two assessments (Figure 4.11) to check specific progress as the children had moved on to Book Band 3.

section four

Running Record Assessment

Text: *Hedgehog is Hungry* by Beverley Randell

Name: Suzy **Date: October 16th**

Running Words 47 Errors 4 Self correction rate 1.5		Accuracy 92%	Errors	Self- correction
Page		E SC	E msv	SC msv
3	✓ ✓ ✓ Winter is here.			
5	✓ ✓ sleeping Hedgehog is asleep.	1	ⓜ ⓢ v	
7	✓ ✓ ✓ Spring is here.			
	✓ ✓ ✓ Hedgehog wakes up.			
9	He sc ✓ ✓ Here comes Hedgehog.	1	ⓜ ⓢ ⓥᵢ	m s ⓥ
11	✓ ✓ sniffing Hedgehog is hungry.	1	ⓜ ⓢ v	
	✓ ✓ ✓ ✓ Here is a snail.			
13	✓ ✓ ✓ Hedgehog is hungry.			
	✓ ✓ ✓ ✓ Here is a worm.			
	✓ ✓ ✓ ✓ Here is a caterpillar.			
15	✓ ✓ ✓ spider Here is a beetle.	1	ⓜ ⓢ v	
	✓ ✓ ✓ ✓ Here is a slug. T	1	m s v	
16	✓ ✓ ✓ ✓ ✓ Hedgehog is hungry in the spring.			
		4 1	4 4 1	0 0 1

Figure 4.5 Suzy's running record assessment

section four assessing reading

	Bradley	**Suzy**
First Level of Analysis *Instructional reading level*	Accuracy level: 47 words read, 4 errors = 1:12 = 92% instructional level. Self-correction rate: 4 uncorrected errors + 1 self-correction = 5 errors altogether. Divide 5 errors by the 1 self-correction = 1:5 This analysis means that Bradley is reading at Book Band 2	Accuracy level: 47 words read, 4 errors = 1:12 = 92% instructional level. Self-correction rate: 4 uncorrected errors + 1 self-correction = 5 errors altogether. Divide 5 errors by the 1 self-correction = 1:5 This analysis means that Suzy is reading at Book Band 2.
Second Level of Analysis *Sources of information used*	Predominantly visual information including for self-correction. Meaning not always attended to. Structure sound when used.	Predominantly meaning and structure with little visual information although self-corrected on known word. Meaning is strong. Structure sound.
Third Level of Analysis *Reading strategies used* *Behaviours*	Visual information leads to self-correction. No evidence of re-reading to confirm or self-correct attempts. Not attempting all unknown words independently - appealing and being told. Not always cross checking meaning with visual information. Reads word by word in a monotone.	Visual information leads to self-correction. No evidence of re-reading to confirm or self-correct attempts. Not cross checking meaning with visual information. Reads word by word in a monotone.

Figure 4.6 Summary of Bradley's and Suzy's assessments

Right: Figure 4.7 Blue group running record assessment summary

section four

Running Record Assessment Summary

Blue Group

Name	Word Test (56 words)	Alphabet (26)	Dictated sentences (28 sounds)	Running record summaries
Suzy	29	29	29	Suzy is predominantly using meaning and structure with little attention to visual information although she did self-correct on a known word. No evidence of re-reading to confirm or self-correct. Not cross checking meaning with visual information. Reads word by word in a monotone.
Bradley	22	22	22	Predominantly visual information including for self-correction. Meaning not always attended but structure sound when used. Visual information leads to self-correction. No evidence of re-reading to confirm or self-correct. Not attempting all unknown words independently - appealing and being told. Not always cross checking meaning with visual information. Reads word by word in a monotone.
Angelica	30	30	30	Angelica is using meaning and structure but not always attending to visual information especially beyond the initial letter. Some attempts at cross checking. No evidence of re-reading to confirm or self-correct. Reading lacks fluency but occasionally, especially during speech, there is some expression.
Eddie	21	21	21	Eddie is using visual information - phoneme by phoneme approach at each error. He tends to neglect meaning but structure is consistent. He is not cross checking meaning and visual information and if his attempts at the visual are unsuccessful he relies on being told. Fluency poor.
Roshan	21	21	21	Roshan is using meaning and some visual information but not usually past the initial letter sound. She is cross checking meaning and visual information, but not consistently. No evidence of re-reading for meaning. Fluency poor.

section four assessing reading

Jan completed a Guided Reading proforma to help her plan for instruction (Figure 4.8).

After six weeks the proforma had a great deal of information about Blue Group's progress (Figure 4.9) and she decided to carry out a further running record assessment on Bradley as she wanted to ensure that he was able to read instructionally at the next band. This would act as a benchmark for the whole group (Figure 4.10). She compared the two assessments (Figure 4.11) to check specific progress as the children had moved on to Book Band 3.

Figure 4.8 Guided Reading planning for Blue Group

Guided Reading Record		
Targets 1. Cross check meaning with visual information. 2. Read fluently - two and three word phrases. 3. Read, on the run, an increasing number of high frequency words. 4. Relate events in stories to personal experiences (text-to-self connections)	**Class** Ladybirds **Group** Blue group **Half Term** Autumn first half **Texts** *Lazy Pig* *The Merry-go-round* *Sally and the Daisy* *Lizard Loses his Tail* *A Home for Little Teddy* *Tom is Brave*	**Prompts** • What would make sense and look right? • Look at the picture, then at the word. • Make your reading sound like a story. • Run the words together. • Is that a little word you know?

Name	Session 1	Session 2	Session 3	Session 4	Session 5	Session 6	Returning to the text
Suzy A.							
Bradley E.							
Angelica D.							
Eddie R.							
Roshan J.							

(See Appendix for photocopiable Planning and Target Setting for Guided Reading proforma).

section four

Figure 4.9 Completed Guided Reading record for Blue Group

Guided Reading Record

Targets
1. Cross check meaning with visual information.
2. Read fluently - two and three word phrases.
3. Read, on the run, an increasing number of high frequency words.
4. Relate events in stories to personal experiences (text-to-self connections)

Class Ladybirds
Group Blue group
Half Term Autumn first half
Texts
Lazy Pig
The Merry-go-round
Sally and the Daisy
Lizard Loses his Tail
A Home for Little Teddy
Tom is Brave

Prompts
- What would make sense and look right?
- Look at the picture, then at the word.
- Make your reading sound like a story.
- Run the words together.
- Is that a little word you know?

Name	Session 1	Session 2	Session 3	Session 4	Session 5	Session 6	Returning to the text
Suzy A.	T1✓ more (V) T2✓ 2 words T4✓	T3✓ look like T4 - vocab	T1✓ sun picture T4✓ page 7	T1✓ pge 13 more (V) T4✓ good connecting	T1✓ page 4 (m)+(V) T4✓	T3 when/sc where T4✓	"I was scared once like lizard" (3)
Bradley E.	T1 over reliant on (V) T2 - more work T4✓	T2✓ 2 words T3 look like T4✓	T1✓ page 7 T4✓	T1✓ page 13 (m) ✓✓ T4✓	T1✓ page 4, T3 (M)+(V) T4✓	T3 In/sc Into I look took T4✓	"I fell over and my mum gave me a plaster" (6)
Angelica D.	T1✓ some (V) T2✓ 3 words T4✓	T2✓ speech good T3 T4✓	T1✓ page 11 daisy T4 -✓	T1✓ pge 3 (m)+(S) T4✓	T1✓ pge 14 (m)+(V) T4✓ b-e-d	T3 have/sc here T4✓	"I wouldn't like to sleep in a cage - it's too cold" (5)
Eddie R.	T1✓ Initial letters T2✓ T4✓	T2 - 2 words T3 ✓ T4 - some vocab	T1✓ pge 11 daisy T4✓	T1 ✓ pge 3 I (M)+(V) whole word T4✓	T1✓ pge 13 (M)+(V) T4✓ Initial lt	T3 when where T4 have here	"I've been to a farm & saw other animals" (1)
Roshan J.	T1✓ Initial ltrs T2✓ 2 words T4✓	T2✓ speech good T3 on sc here T4✓	T1✓ page 7 good T4✓ connections	T1 pge 11 (m)+ Initial T4✓	T1✓ page 4 (M)+(V) T4✓	T3✓ all correct good T4✓ connector	"I got my mum a flower too" (2)

section four assessing reading

Running Record Assessment

Text: *Little Rabbit's Party* by Jenny Giles

Name: Bradley   **Date:** October 20th

Running Words 98 Errors 6 Self correction rate 1.5	Accuracy 92%	Errors	Self-correction

Page		E	SC	E msv	SC msv
2	✓ ✓ ✓ ✓ ✓ ✓ Little Duck went for a walk.				
	A SC ✓ ✓ ✓ ✓ "I will go and see	1		ⓜⓢ v	m s ⓥ
	✓ ✓ ✓ ✓ Little Kitten today," T she said.	1		m s v?	
4	✓ ✓ ✓ ✓ ✓ ✓ Little Duck said to Little Kitten				
	✓ ✓ ✓ ✓ ✓ ✓ ✓ "Will you come and play with me?"				
	Will SC ✓ ✓ Little Kitten said,	1		ⓜⓢ v	m s ⓥ
6	✓ ✓ ✓ ✓ ✓ ✓ "I can not play with you.				
	✓ ✓ ✓✓ birthday ✓ "I'm going to a - party.	1			ⓜⓢ v i/m
	✓✓✓ Rabbit to "It is Little Rabbit's birthday T today."	3		{ ⓜⓢⓥ m s v? m ⓢⓥᵢ	
	On ✓ ✓ ✓ "Oh," said Little Duck.	1		m ⓢⓥᵢ	
8	✓ ✓ ✓ ✓ ✓ ✓ "I'm not going to the party.				
	✓✓ ✓ ✓ ✓ I will go back home."				
10	✓ ✓ ✓ ✓✓ birthday ✓ Little Kitten went to the - party.	1		ⓜⓢ v	
	✓ ✓ ✓ ✓ ✓ And Little Duck went home.				
12	✓ ✓ ✓ ✓ On the way home,				

section four

Page		E	SC	E msv	SC msv
14	✓ ✓ ✓ Little Duck said, ✓ ✓ ✓ ✓ ✓ "I can see Little Rabbit." ✓ ✓ ✓ ✓ Ducks ✓ ✓ Little Rabbit said, "Little Duck! Little duck! ✓ ✓ ✓ ✓ "I'm looking for you."	1		ⓜⓢⓥ i/m	
		8	2	5 8 4	0 0 2

Figure 4.10 Bradley's second running record assessment

Jan decided that in order to move Blue Group forward, she would need to concentrate on developing reading strategies especially orchestrating all sources of information by reading on and re-reading. Further work on fluency would be needed in order to tackle longer phrases and sentences.

section four assessing reading

	Bradley's first reading record assessment *Hedgehog is Hungry*	**Bradley's second reading record assessment** *Little Rabbit's Party*
First Level of Analysis *Instructional reading level*	Accuracy level: 47 words read, 4 errors = 1:12 = 92% instructional level. Self-correction rate: 4 uncorrected errors + 1 self-correction = 5 errors altogether. Divide 5 errors by the 1 self-correction =1:5 This analysis means that Bradley is Reading at Book Band 2.	Accuracy level: 98 words read, 8 errors = 1:12.25 = 92% instructional level. Self-correction rate: 8 uncorrected errors + 2 self-corrections = 10 errors altogether. Divide 10 errors by the 2 self-correction = 1:5 This analysis means that Bradley is reading at Book Band 3.
Second Level of Analysis *Sources of information used*	Predominantly visual information including for self-correction. Meaning not always attended to. Structure sound when used.	Predominantly structure and some meaning as well as visual cues used when attempting challenging words. Attention to initial and sometimes middle visual information.
Third Level of Analysis *Reading strategies used* *Behaviours*	Visual information leads to self-correction. No evidence of re-reading to confirm or self-correct attempts. Not attempting all unknown words independently - appealing and being told. Not always cross-checking meaning with visual information. Reads word by word in a monotone.	More visual information leads to two self-corrections. No evidence of re-reading to confirm or self-correct attempts. Not attempting all unknown words independently. Reads two and three word phrases fluently.

Figure 4.11 Comparison of Bradley's first and second running record assessments

The phonics check

One of the most powerful aspects of running record assessments is the information they give teachers about independent application of taught skills - about children's ability to orchestrate all aspects of reading.

The phonics screening test administered at the end of Year 1 merely assesses children's ability to blend phonemes in sequence to decode words and non-words. This does not give information about children's ability to read.

Although there is a need to prepare children for the phonics check, there is no better way than providing quality teaching. It may be useful to give practice tests so that the children become familiar with the format but this should be done near the date of the test and not continually throughout the year.

In summary

As teachers develop their understanding of the assessment process, so too they develop their subject knowledge - their understanding of how children pick up and process print.

Rigorous assessment is a vital cog in the cycle of reading instruction and in order to move children forward as readers, teachers need, through running records, a diagnostic analysis of what children are able to do and what they need support to achieve. This is particularly so for lower attaining pupils where unpicking what is getting 'in the way' is even more crucial to ensuring progress. Alongside this, detailed teacher assessment through observations during Guided and other reading sessions will not only help to keep track of individual progress but also give valuable information about progress across a class or year group.

Keeping careful records and using these to inform planning is a key professional skill. The most useful assessments are those which lead children's learning forward. In addition, parents and learners themselves should feel that any comments on progress are positive and will lead to greater success and satisfaction in learning. Reading is more than a core skill in the primary curriculum; it can offer lifelong pleasure and satisfaction.If children are to become keen and committed readers then they need a secure and carefully monitored start.

Alongside formal assessments, daily observation of children as they engage with books, choose according to their preferences or follow a favourite author, will also help teachers provide rich reading opportunities. Discussions about books, an enthusiastic teacher who enjoys reading, and makes sensitive suggestions about where to go next are essential to the provision of a good reading environment. These informal assessment opportunities also contribute to professional knowledge about how best to teach, assess and plan for reading progress.

references

Assessment Reform Group (2012) Assessment for learning: 10 principles. Available online at: www.assessment-reform-group.org Accessed 26th April, 2015.

Chambers, A. (2011) *Tell Me (Children, Reading & Talk) with the Reading Environment*. Stroud, Glos: Thimble Press.

Bodman, S. and Franklin, G. (eds) (2014) *Which Book and Why*. London: Institute of Education Press.

BFI Education (2003) *Starting Stories: A Film and Literacy Resource for Three- to Seven-year-olds*. London: British Film Institute.

Bussis, A., Chittenden, E., Amarel, M. and Klausner, E. (1985) *Inquiry into Meaning: An investigation of learning to read*. Princeton NJ: Lawrence Erlbaum Associates.

Caravette, L. (2011) Portrait of the Reader as a Young Child. *Children & Libraries: The Journal of the Association for Library Service to Children*, 9 (2) pp. 52-57.

Clark, M. (2014) *Learning to be Literate: insights from research for policy and practice*. Birmingham: Glendale Education.

Clay, M. (1991) *Becoming Literate: the construction of inner control*. Portsmouth, New Hampshire: Heinemann.

Clay, M. (2006) *An Observation Survey of Early Literacy Achievement*. Portsmouth, New Hampshire: Heinemann.

Clay, M. (2008) *Literacy Lessons Designed for Individuals, Part Two, Teaching Procedures*. Rosedale, NZ. Heinemann/Pearson.

Courtney, A. and Gleeson, M., (2007) *Building Bridges of Understanding: a whole school approach to the teaching of comprehension*. The manual can be bought by visiting: http://www.cdu.mic.ul.ie/Newresource/default.html

Department for Education (2013) *National curriculum in England: English programmes of study*. https://www.gov.uk/government/publications/national-curriculum-in-england-english-programmes-of-study/national-curriculum-in-england-english-programmes-of-study Accessed 26th April, 2015

Department for Education (2104) *Statutory framework for the early years foundation stage: Setting the standards for learning, development and care for children from birth to five*. https://www.gov.uk/government/uploads/system/uploads/attachment_data/file/335504/EYFS_framework_from_1_September_2014__with_clarification_note.pdf Accessed 26th April, 2015

Department for Education and Employment (1998) *The National Literacy Strategy: Framework for Teaching*. Crown Copyright.

Department for Education and Skills (2007) Letters and Sounds: Notes of Guidance for Practitioners and Teachers. Available on http://www.teachfind.com/national-strategies/letters-and-sounds-notes-guidance-practitioners-and-teachers Accessed 26th April, 2015.

Department for Education and Skills (2007) *Letters and Sounds: Principles and Practice of High Quality Phonics*. Available on: https://www.gov.uk/government/uploads/system/uploads/attachment_data/file/190599/Letters_and_Sounds_-_DFES-00281-2007.pdf Accessed 26th April, 2015.

Dombey, H. (2010) with assistance from Bearne, E., Cremin, T., Ellis, S., Mottram, M., O'Sullivan, O., Öztürk, A., Reedy, D. of UKLA and Raphael, T. and Allington, R. of the International Reading Association *Teaching Reading: What the evidence says*. Leicester: United Kingdom Literacy Association.

Fountas, I.C. and Pinnell, G.S. (1996) *Guided reading: Good first teaching for all children*. Portsmouth, New Hampshire: Heinemann.

references

Goodwin, P. (2014) 'Great Books for Great Readers'. Talk given to United Kingdom Literacy Association International Conference, Brighton.

Gough, P.B. and Tunmer, W.E. (1986) 'Decoding, reading and reading disability', *Remedial and Special Education*, 7 pp. 6-10.

Government of South Australia Department for Education and Child Development, Literacy Secretariat (2014) *Engaging in and Exploring Running Records*. Available on: http://www.decd.sa.gov.au/northernadelaide/files/links/DECD_Running_Records_1_v8.pdf Accessed 26th April, 2015

Hildreth, G. (1959) Reading and the language arts, *Education* pp. 565-569.

Iaquinta, A. (2006) Guided Reading: A Research-Based Response to the Challenges of Early Reading Instruction, *Early Childhood Education Journal* 33 (6) pp. 413-418.

Juel, C. and Minden-Cupp, C. (2001) Learning to read words: linguistic units and instructional strategies, *Reading Research Quarterly* 35 (4) pp. 458-493. Literacy Shed website https://www.google.co.uk/?gws_rd=ssl#q=Literacy+Shed+

Mallett, M. (2005) Early Years Reading: from hornbooks to electronic texts, in *Books for Keeps* No. 150. http://booksforkeeps.co.uk/issue/150/childrens-books/articles/other-articles/early-years-reading-from-hornbooks-to-electronic Accessed 26th April, 2015

Morrison, I. (1994) *Keeping It Together: Linking Reading Theory and Practice*. Mishawaka, IN: The Wright Group.

Palincsar, A.S. (1986) *Reciprocal teaching. Teaching reading as thinking*. Oak Brook, IL: North Central Regional Educational Laboratory.

Palincsar, A., Brown, A and Campione, J. (1993) First Grade Dialogues for Knowledge Acquisition and Use, in E. Forman, N. Minick and C. Addison Stone *Contexts for Learning: Sociocultural Dynamics in Children's Development*. Oxford: Oxford University Press pp. 43-57.

Pardo, L.S. (2004) What every teacher needs to know about comprehension, in *The Reading Teacher*, 5 (3) pp. 272-280.

Randall, B., Giles, J. and Smith, A. (1996) *Dressing-Up*. Rigby PM Collection. Boston, Mass: Houghton Mifflin Harcourt Publishing Company.

Rose, J. (2006) *The independent review of the teaching of early reading*. Nottingham: DfES.

Smith, F. (1978) *Reading without Nonsense*. New York: Teachers College Press.

Trelease, J. (2013) *The Read Aloud Handbook* 7th edition. New York: Penguin Books.

list of children's books

Jez Alborough (2013) *Six Little Chicks*. Red Fox Picture Books. ISBN 978 1 84941611 5

Graham Baker-Smith (2009) *Leon and the Place Between*. Templar. ISBN 978 1 84011801 8

Quentin Blake (2012) *Mrs Armitage Queen of The Road*. Jonathan Cape. ISBN 978 0 09943424 5

Raymond Briggs (1963) *Jim and the Beanstalk*. Puffin Picture Books. ISBN 978 0 14050077 6

Anthony Browne (2008) *The Tunnel*. Walker Books. ISBN 978 1 40631329 1

Eileen Browne (2006) *Handa's Surprise*. Walker Books. ISBN 978 0 74453634 8

John Burningham (2001) *Mr Gumpy's Outing*. Red Fox. ISBN 978 0 09940879 6

Eric Carle (1994) *The Very Hungry Caterpillar*. Philomel Publication. ISBN 978 0 39922690 8

Caroline Jayne Church (2003) *Do Your Ears Hang Low?* Chicken House. ISBN 978 0 43912871 1

Babette Cole (1996) *Princess Smartypants*. Puffin. ISBN 978 0 14055526 4

Helen Cooper (2008) *The Bear Under the Stairs*. Picture Corgi. ISBN 978 0 55255845 7

Helen Cooper (1999) *Pumpkin Soup*. Corgi Childrens. ISBN 978 0 55254510 5

June Crebbin (1996) illustrated Stephen Lambert *The Train Ride*. Walker Books. ISBN 978 8 96224556 1

Andy Cutbill (2011) illustrated Russell Ayto *First Week at Cow School*. HarperCollins. ISBN 978 0 00727468 0

Roald Dahl (2007) illustrated Quentin Blake *The BFG*. Puffin. ISBN 978 0 14132262 9

Julia Donaldson (2002) illustrated Axel Scheffler *The Smartest Giant in Town*. Macmillan Children's Books. ISBN 978 0 33396144 5

Julia Donaldson (2002) *Room on the Broom*. Macmillan Children's Books. ISBN 978 0 33390338 4

Jacqui Farley (1994) illustrated Pamela Venus *Giant Hiccups*. Tamarind. ISBN 978 1 87051627 3

Michael Foreman/Oscar Wilde (1982) illustrated Michael Foreman and Freire Wright *The Selfish Giant*. Picture Puffin. ISBN 978 0 14050383 8

Emily Gravett (2008) *Monkey and Me*. Macmillan Children's Books. ISBN 978 0 23001583 8

Mini Grey (2006) *Traction Man is Here*. Red Fox. ISBN 978 0 09945109 9

Mini Grey (2007) *The Adventures of The Dish And The Spoon*. Red Fox. ISBN 978 0 09947576 7

Mary Hoffman (reissue 2007) *Amazing Grace*. Frances Lincoln. ISBN 978 1 84507749 5

Mary Hoffman (1997) *Grace and Family*. Frances Lincoln. ISBN 978 0 71120869 8

Shirley Hughes (2002) *Dogger*. Red Fox. ISBN 978 0 09992790 7

Pat Hutchins (1998) *Rosie's Walk*. Red Fox. ISBN 978 0 37032446 3

David McKee (1989) *Elmer*. HarperCollins. ISBN 978 0 68809171 2

David McKee (2012) *Not Now Bernard*. Andersen. ISBN 978 1 84939467 3

David Mills (1999) *Lima's Red Hot Chilli* (in Arabic and English). Mantra Lingua. ISBN 978 1 85269420 3

Tony Mitton (2002) *Down by the Cool of the Pool*. Orchard Books. ISBN 978 1 84121098 8

list of children's books

Jill Murphy (Reissue 2013) *The Worst Witch*. Puffin. ISBN 978 0 14134959 6

Jill Murphy (2007) *Whatever Next?* Pan Macmillan. ISBN 978 0 23001547 0

Jan Oke (2005) *The Naughty Bus*. Little Knowall Publishing. ISBN 978 0 95479211 4

Hiawyn Oram and Satoshi Kitamura (1982) *Angry Arthur*. Andersen. ISBN 978 0 86264017 0

Marcus Pfister trans. J. Alison James (1998) *The Rainbow Fish*. North South Books. ISBN 978 1 55858009 1

Martin Waddell (1995) illustrated Helen Oxenbury *Farmer Duck*. Walker Books. ISBN 978 0 74453660 7

Martin Waddell (1996) illustrated Patrick Benson *Owl Babies*. Walker Books. ISBN 978 0 74454923 2

Martin Waddell (2006) illustrated Jill Barton *The Pig in the Pond*. Walker Books. ISBN 978 1 40630540 1

Jenny Wagner (1979) illustrated Ron Brooks John Brown, *Rose and the Midnight Cat*. Puffin Books. ISBN 978 0 14050306 7

Richard Walker (2006) illustrated Niamh Sharkey *Jack and the Beanstalk*. Barefoot Books. ISBN 978 1 90523669 5

Margaret Wild (2006) illustrated Ron Brooks *Fox*. Turtleback Books. ISBN 978 1 41774997 3

Brian Wildsmith (1982) *Cat on the Mat*. Oxford University Press. ISBN 978 0 19272123 5

Mo Willems (2004) *Don't Let the Pigeon Drive the Bus*. Walker Books. ISBN 978 1 84428513 6

Jeanne Willis (2005) illustrated Tony Ross *Tadpole's Promise*. Andersen. ISBN 978 1 84270426 4

glossary

Analytic phonics refers to an approach where the sounds associated with letters are not pronounced in isolation but children identify phonic elements for words which each contain a similar element, either at the start of the word - onset - or in the later part of the word - rime. So to read the word 'cat' would require children to recognise the rime 'at' and then add the onset 'c'.

Blending Recognising the letter sounds in a written word, for example c-u-p and merging or synthesising them in the order in which they are written to pronounce the word 'cup'.

Digraph Two letters which make one sound. A consonant digraph contains two consonants: sh ck th ll. A vowel digraph contains at least one vowel: ai ee ar oy.

Grapheme Letter(s) representing a phoneme.

Graphophonic Graphophonic cues involve the letter-sound or sound-symbol relationships of language.

Morpheme The smallest meaningful unit in a language.

Onset and rime A syllable can normally be divided into two parts: the onset, which consists of the initial consonant or consonant blend, and the rime which consists of the vowel and any final consonants.

Oral blending Hearing a series of spoken sounds and merging them together to make a spoken word – no text is used, for example, when a teacher calls out 'b-u-s', the children say 'bus'. This skill is usually taught before blending and reading printed words.

Phoneme The smallest unit of sound in a word.

Segmenting Identifying the individual sounds in a spoken word (e.g. h-i-m) and writing down or manipulating letters for each sound to form the word 'him'.

Semantic Related to meaning.

Split digraph A digraph in which the two letters are not adjacent: m a k e

Syntax The study of the principles and processes by which sentences are constructed in a language.

Syntactic Related to grammatical sentence structure.

Synthetic phonics An approach in which the sounds identified with letters are learned in isolation and blended together, for example, a synthetic approach to reading 'cat' would require children to decode the word phoneme by phoneme 'c-a-t'.

Trigraph Three letters which make one sound: igh dge

Appendix / Photocopiable Resources

Early concepts about print: opportunities for assessment

Early Concept	Prompts	Assessment Opportunities
Recognise one or two words in different contexts.	• Can you find your name? • Is that a little word you know?	• Finding names, e.g. register, pegs, name cards, names on alphabet • Flash cards - whole class/school assessment • Reading written texts
Understand and use simple terminology such as book, right way up, front, back, upside down.	• Put the book on the stand. • Show me the front of the book. • Take a book from the table.	• Shared Reading • Individual Reading • Observations
Understand that print goes from left to right including return sweep.	• Where do I start to read? • Show me where to start reading. • Where do I go after that?	• Shared Reading • Individual Reading • Shared Writing
Understand that the left page comes before the right. *NB print must be on both pages when assessing this.*	• Where do I start to read? • Show me where to start reading. • Where do I go after that?	• Shared Reading • Shared Writing
Know that print (not the picture) tells the story.	• Where do I start to read? • Show me where to start reading. • Where do I go after that?	• Shared Reading • Individual Reading
Know that there are letters, and clusters of letters called words.	• Show me the first letter. • Show me the last letter. • Show me a capital letter. • Show me one word.	• Using magnetic letters to make words - put words into context • Shared Reading • Individual Reading • Shared Writing
Understand that there are first letters and last letters in words.	• Show me the first letter. • Show me the last letter. • Show me a capital letter. • Show me one word.	• Shared Reading • Guided Reading • Individual Reading
Match one to one.	• Point to the words as I read them. • Match the counters to the words. • Use your pointing finger.	• Individual Reading (using the pointing finger) • Group/Guided Reading • Cut up sentences • Moving counters to match words

© United Kingdom Literacy Association *Teaching Early Reading: More Than Phonics* 2015. (Drawn from the work of Marie Clay).

Intervention for reading difficulties

Name:

Class:

Date:

Indicator	Comments
Does not use meaning as a source of information.	
Has poor word level skills.	
Has poor phonological awareness.	
Has difficulty with recall of high frequency words.	
Is over reliant on being 'told' words rather than having strategies to problem solve.	
Reads slowly giving the same weight to each word.	
Reads without fluency or expression.	
Often finger points.	
Has limited vocabulary.	
Lacks real or imagined experiences to bring to a text.	
Has poor grammatical skills.	
Is over reliant on one source of information. (Indicate which)	
Is over reliant on one strategy. (Indicate which)	

Planned interventions:

Time frame:

Outcomes:

Planning and Target Setting for Guided Reading *Emergent/Early*

Class: Group: Date (half term):

Highlight half termly targets to indicate teaching focus

Emergent	**Early**
Pre band 1, Bands 1 and 2	**Bands 3, 4, 5, 6**

• read and understand simple sentences
• demonstrate understanding when talking with others about what they have read
• recognise one or two words in different contexts
• understand and use simple terminology such as book, right way up, front, back, upside down
• understand that print goes from left to right including return sweep
• understand that the left page comes before the right
• know that print (not the picture) tells the story
• know that there are letters, and clusters of letters called words
• understand that there are first letters and last letters in words
• match one to one.
	• know that print conveys meaning - what they read makes sense
	• know how language is written down: the grammatical structure, including punctuation - what they read sounds right grammatically
	• know about visual information:
	  - phonics
	  - graphic information including word endings and words of more than one syllable
	  - know and apply of a range of reading strategies:
	  - self-monitoring
	  - self-correcting
	  - orchestrating all sources of information
	  - cross checking meaning and visual information.

• express themselves effectively, showing awareness of listeners' needs • use vocabulary and forms of speech that are increasingly influenced by their experience of books • use simple grammatical structures orally.	• read fluently • read with expression.

• understand literally what has been read and sequence key events
• reach a deeper understanding of what has been read by using a range of reading comprehension strategies:
  - summarising (retelling)
  - predicting (before reading)
  - visualising (simple settings)
  - questioning (responding)
  - connecting (text-to-self).
	• understand literally what has been read and sequence key events
	• reach a deeper understanding of what has been read by using a range of reading comprehension strategies:
	  - summarising (key events)
	  - predicting (before and during reading)
	  - visualising (settings)
	  - questioning (responding and generating)
	  - connecting (text-to-self, text-to-text)
	• understand and describe information.

Texts	**Prompts**

Name	Session 1	Session 2	Session 3	Session 4	Session 5	Session 6	Response to text

© United Kingdom Literacy Association *Teaching Early Reading: More Than Phonics* 2015.

Planning and Target Setting for Guided Reading *Early/Transitional*

Class: Group: Date (half term):

Highlight half termly targets to indicate teaching focus

Early	**Transitional**
Bands 3, 4, 5, 6	
• know that print conveys meaning - what they read makes sense • know how language is written down: the grammatical structure, including punctuation - what they read sounds right grammatically • know about visual information: 　- phonics 　- graphic information including word endings and words of more than one syllable 　- know and apply of a range of reading strategies: 　- self-monitoring 　- self-correcting 　- orchestrating all sources of information cross checking meaning and visual information.	• use context of what they read to decode • control more complex and varied grammatical structures • use a wider range of visual information including prefixes, suffixes and syllabification • know and apply of a range of reading strategies: 　- self-monitoring 　- self-correcting 　- orchestrating all sources of information 　- re-reading 　- reading on.
• read fluently • read with expression	• read fluently • read with expression • begin to read silently.
• understand literally what has been read and sequence key events 　- reach a deeper understanding of what has been read by using a range of reading comprehension strategies: 　- summarising (key events) 　- predicting (before and during reading) 　- visualising (settings) 　- questioning (responding and generating) 　- connecting (text-to-self, text-to-text) • understand and describe information.	• reach a deeper understanding of what has been read by using a range of reading comprehension strategies: 　- summarising (key events) 　- predicting (before, during and after reading) 　- visualising (settings, characters) 　- questioning (responding and generating) 　- connecting (text-to-self, text-to-text, text-to-world) 　- inferring (reading between the lines) • understand, describe, select or retrieve information.
Texts	**Prompts**

Name	Session 1	Session 2	Session 3	Session 4	Session 5	Session 6	Response to text

© United Kingdom Literacy Association *Teaching Early Reading: More Than Phonics* 2015.

Planning and Target Setting for Guided Reading *Transitional/ Self-extending*

Class: Group: Date (half term):

Highlight half termly targets to indicate teaching focus

Transitional	Self-extending
Bands 7, 8, 9	**Band 10**

• use context of what they read to decode
• control more complex and varied grammatical structures
• use a wider range of visual information including prefixes, suffixes and syllabification
• know and apply of a range of reading strategies:
  - self-monitoring
  - self-correcting
  - orchestrating all sources of information
  - re-reading
  - reading on.
	• use context of what they read to decode
	• control more complex and varied grammatical structures
	• use a wider range of visual information including prefixes, suffixes and syllabification
	• know and apply of a range of reading strategies:
	  - self-monitoring
	  - self-correcting
	  - orchestrating all sources of information
	  - re-reading
	  - reading on.

• read fluently • read with expression • begin to read silently.	• read fluently • read with expression • read silently.

• reach a deeper understanding of what has been read by using a range of reading comprehension strategies:
  - summarising (key events)
  - predicting (before, during and after reading)
  - visualising (settings, characters)
  - questioning (responding and generating)
  - connecting (text-to-self, text-to-text, text-to-world)
  - inferring (reading between the lines)
• understand, describe, select or retrieve information.
	• reach a deeper understanding of what has been read by using a range of reading comprehension strategies:
	  - summarising (key events)
	  - predicting (before, during and after reading)
	  - visualising (settings, characters)
	  - questioning (responding and generating)
	  - connecting (text-to-self, text-to-text, text-to-world)
	  - inferring (reading between the lines)
	• understand, describe, select or retrieve information, events or ideas from texts and begin to use quotations and references from the text.
	• explain and comment on writers' use of language, including some grammatical and some literary features.
	• identify and comment on writers' purposes and viewpoints and the overall effect of the text on the reader.
	• relate texts to their social, cultural and historical contexts.

Texts	**Prompts**

Name	Session 1	Session 2	Session 3	Session 4	Session 5	Session 6	Response to text

© United Kingdom Literacy Association *Teaching Early Reading: More Than Phonics* 2015.